David Bradley's *No Place to Hide, 1*
succinct and straightforward account
quences of our nuclear capability. Hi
universal danger of radiation is even more compelling
today than when it was first published. Now updated,
the book's final message is urgently clear: we must halt
our mindless race towards a nuclear holocaust in which
we all may perish.

—SENATOR ALAN CRANSTON, *California*

No Place to Hide, 1946/1984, is a very important book.
It is essential that every person in this society understand
the medical consequences of nuclear war so that their
psychic numbing can be discarded in favor of fear, de-
pression and moral outrage, then activism.

—HELEN CALDICOTT, M.D., *President,
Physicians for Social Responsibility*

When I first read this book, I believed that its clear and
forceful message would help to persuade mankind that a
nuclear war was unthinkable. Instead, we have witnessed
a build-up of nuclear weapons that no one had dreamed
of — even in his worst nightmare. Therefore the message
of the book is even more important today.

—JOHN G. KEMENY, *President Emeritus,
Dartmouth College, and Chairman,
President's Commission on the
Accident at Three Mile Island*

Few world leaders have ever seen a nuclear explosion or witnessed the human tragedy of Hiroshima and Nagasaki. In *No Place to Hide, 1946/1984*, a firsthand account of the relatively "small" atomic tests at Bikini in 1946, Dr. David Bradley has made understandable for all of us the magnitude of destruction caused by nuclear weapons.

—ERIC CHIVIAN, M.D.
*International Physicians for
Prevention of Nuclear War*

David Bradley's *No Place to Hide* was really an early warning about the nuclear threat to humanity, but few people were listening. Now he has written an epilogue that speaks even more eloquently about what has happened since his early and unheeded warning. Books like Dr. Bradley's are a sincere effort to replace the present insanity with reason and faith in our power to control and unmake the monster we have created before it is used, even accidentally, to undo the beautiful works of God's creation and our own. This is no longer an early warning; the scientists themselves tell us it is four minutes to midnight, a brief moment in which to decide whether our world and ourselves will survive in peace or be utterly exterminated in a horrible holocaust. This is the most devastating moral problem that has ever faced humankind on earth. There is no place to hide.

— FATHER THEODORE HESBURGH, *President,
University of Notre Dame*

No Place to Hide

1946/1984

No Place to Hide
1946/1984

DAVID BRADLEY

Foreword by Jerome B. Wiesner

PUBLISHED FOR DARTMOUTH COLLEGE
BY UNIVERSITY PRESS OF NEW ENGLAND
HANOVER AND LONDON

UNIVERSITY PRESS OF NEW ENGLAND

BRANDEIS UNIVERSITY
BROWN UNIVERSITY
CLARK UNIVERSITY
DARTMOUTH COLLEGE
UNIVERSITY OF NEW HAMPSHIRE
UNIVERSITY OF RHODE ISLAND
TUFTS UNIVERSITY
UNIVERSITY OF VERMONT

Library of Congress Cataloging in Publication data will be found on the last printed page of this book.

Printed in the United States of America

89 88 87 86 85 84 83   8 7 6 5 4 3 2 1

PHOTOGRAPH CREDITS

Following p. 89:
July 1, 1946. Bikini Atoll: National Archives, 80-G-478061.
The fireball rising: National Archives, 306-NJ-1344C-1.
Diver with geiger probe: National Archives, CR-990-1.
Bikini wrasse: Dr. Loren Donaldson, University of Washington.

Following p. 114:
The four photographs: National Archives, RG-374.

Following p. 168:
August 6, 1945: Air Force Photo, 1945.
1945: National Archives, 243-NP-I-35.
1946: Author's collection.
1953: Defense Audiovisual Agency, Navy, K-26354.
1956: National Archives, 80-G-698209.

To Kim, Darby, Wendy, Ben,
Bronwen, and Steve

So shall you hear
Of carnal, bloody, and unnatural acts;
Of accidental judgments, casual slaughters;
Of deaths put on by cunning and forc'd cause;
And, in this upshot, purposes mistook
Fall'n on th' inventors' heads.

— Horatio in *Hamlet*, Act 5, Scene 2

They trow not what is shaping otherwhere
The while they talk thus stoutly.

— Spirit of the Years in *The Dynasts*,
by Thomas Hardy

CONTENTS

FOREWORD

THIS LITTLE BOOK, *No Place to Hide, 1946/1984,* published originally more than a quarter of a century and five trillion dollars' worth of weapons ago, was prompted by the first peacetime test of nuclear weapons, conducted off the shore of the Pacific island of Bikini. It is frightening evidence of humanity's inability to compromise and choose rational alternatives even in the face of impending doom. In fact, people will not even consider the possibility of inevitable doom. After the annihilation of Hiroshima and Nagasaki, the cliché expressed by experts and laymen alike was that the new force released by splitting the atom increased so enormously the means of destruction that war was obsolete, that atomic weapons were so powerful that they had no real military use, and that wars between states possessing them was too horrible to contemplate. It was also believed that because atomic weapons cause such inhumane conditions, they would never again be used. So far nuclear weapons have not been used again, but there is the constant threat of their use against civilian populations, and their numbers grow right along with the escalating fear of nuclear war.

It is an almost universal belief that the world cannot long survive on the present course, a belief reinforced by the more than thousandfold increase in the effectiveness of nuclear weapons. Yet in both the United States and the Soviet Union a mixture of fear, secrecy, technical arrogance, faulty military doctrine, ignorance, bureaucratic momentum, and outright falsehoods has sustained and fed a hopeless search for security through the ceaseless outpouring of more deadly weapons. This is madness on a global scale. Its current manifestation in the United States is the war-winning plans of the Reagan administration and in the Soviet Union the vast buildup of the SS-20.

As Dr. Bradley watched two primitive atomic bombs destroy battle-tested naval ships and recalled the devastation similar weapons had caused at Hiroshima and Nagasaki, he realized that every city in the world and all of their inhabitants would soon become helpless hostages unless the bomb could be eliminated. There would be literally no place to hide.

The evidence was really there before the Bikini tests. They were merely exclamation marks that should have driven home for everyone and for all time that simple truth. The evidence is conclusive. A few dozen nuclear weapons will destroy a modern society.

Up to now the superpowers have ignored this basic fact and piled up thousands of nuclear weapons and sophisticated delivery systems, only making more certain that there is no escape. Equally absurd, both sides continue to look for the impossible — for defensive systems capable of preventing even a miniscule part of these incomprehensible stockpiles from exploding on their cities.

Eventually each United States president and Soviet leader in the nuclear age has come to realize that nuclear bombs are not usable except as a threat, and so each has turned to a search for ways to moderate the danger. So far none has succeeded. Even the Reagan administration is learning this lesson. It came into office intent upon building a "war-fighting capability." This unachievable goal was a reaction to a vast Soviet missile buildup. But the Soviet buildup, we like to forget, was a reaction to the earlier United States deployment of land-based missiles, missile-carrying submarines, MIRVs, and the continuing development of new weapons systems. In any event, we can hope that President Reagan, like his predecessors, will come to believe the lesson that Dr. Bradley tried to teach us so long ago: the choice is between continued civilization or annihilation by nuclear war.

Why won't the lesson, so obvious after the surprisingly devastating explosions at Bikini, stay learned? Why is it that the impossibility of winning a nuclear war, intuitively so clear to the average layman, has to be learned again and again with each change of leadership? I am convinced that this is the consequence of two facts: the enormous influence wielded by the defense establishments of the superpowers and the fact that there are no experts on nuclear war.

The first is self-evident: the military departments of the two contestants in the arms race are by many times the largest bureaucratic establishments the world has ever known. Second, while technical experts invent, design, and manufacture the weapon systems, defense establishments have no consistent method for fitting strategies and tactics to their new arms. Moreover, since defense experts fear that they will be blamed for any loophole, real or imaginary, in the nation's defenses, they exaggerate the dangers and inflate their demands for new weapons.

Such a fluid doctrinal situation, combined with the bureaucratic drive for survival and growth, creates a lust for new weapons and a constantly changing policy to justify them. Just this syndrome was discussed at length by General Thomas Jones, recent head of the Joint Chiefs of Staff, in a *New York Times* article in the fall of 1981, soon after he retired. I could not prove that the Soviet Union suffers from exactly the same pressures for military expansion, but seen from the outside it manifests all of the same symptoms.

But no one knows how to use nuclear weapons. While there are thousands of experts on technical matters and hardware, on the critical issues of strategy, tactics, deterrents, war-winning, etc., there are truly no experts. *None!* No one knows for sure about the actual field performance of missiles or their accuracy and reliability.

Because it is impossible to test nuclear weapon systems, uncertainty about their performance in combat predominates even more than for individual components.

Clearly then, a nuclear weapon system must be viewed with much skepticism. But military doctrine relating to strategy and tactics involving nuclear weapons is even more ephemeral. There has never been a war — even a tiny one — where tactical or strategic nuclear weapons were available to both sides. Planners are, therefore, completely dependent on theory to support their strategies. Analysts and military officers who plan for the use of conventional weapons can draw on past experience as well as conduct more or less realistic field exercises to test their ideas about new or improved tactics or weapons. But because there has never been a nuclear war or even one nuclear weapon fired at another, all of the scenarios spoken with such solemnity by so-called experts are based entirely on speculation. Nuclear arms strategies are products of the imagination of analysts and military officers whose impossible professional challenge is to figure out how to fight and win a nuclear war.

Our defense planners face an unanswerable question right at the start: What does winning a nuclear war mean? Getting in the last blow? Having only 100 million dead compared to the 120 million for the opponent? Having more weapons left over after a massive exchange?

Because nuclear weapons have not been used in combat, any prediction about the outcome of a nuclear war is based entirely on assumptions. To be sure the analysts use computer models as a substitute for field exercises, but the predictions from such models are totally dependent on the assumptions — guesses — put into the models by these same analysts. Such questions as the reliability of missiles when operated by soldiers instead of trained technicians and fired by the hundreds or thousands instead of singly, the reliability of the command and control system, the accuracy of guidance systems, certain knowledge about the location of all the opponent's weapons, and validity of estimates of target vulnerability are among the many unknowable factors.

Even when computer models are used to design relatively simple physical systems such as power systems, aircraft, or computers, a certain amount of trial and error must correct for unanticipated deficiencies. But how can this method apply to modeling a massive nuclear war in which there probably will only be one trial? I doubt that the citizens of the United States or the Soviet Union would agree to rerun a nuclear war to take advantage of the experience gained in the first one.

Now even the Reagan administration agrees that the only role for nuclear weapons is as a deterrent, that is, to prevent their use by someone else. In a recent position paper to Congress, the Joint Chiefs of Staff stated that their main goal was to build an adequate deterrent. Unfortunately, their definition of such a deterrent included the capability to fight and win a nuclear war.

The issue finally boils down to what is an adequate deterrent? Here we have entered into a realm where facts are nonexistent and opinions and emotions dominate. What level of retaliatory capability is required to deter a Soviet strike on the United States? What percentage of destruction would the Soviet leaders be willing to accept in order to win a nuclear war? Ten percent? Twenty percent? Forty or fifty percent? Who knows? Probably not even they. Many people, myself included, do not believe that the Soviet leaders would risk the destruction of their society in order to accomplish even major political or military gains. Others, including some of our political leaders and their advisers, believe the Soviet Union would accept enormous punishment if it achieved some sort of world domination. It is hard to understand how a totally destroyed Soviet Union could rule the world or why it would matter much to an equally devastated Europe or United States.

No one can read the minds of the Soviet leaders. Thus the predictions of Soviet intentions, so important in determining United States military posture, are even less well-founded than the war-fighting scenarios.

Because there is no way to resolve strategic questions, the so-called experts tend to be extremely doctrinaire. Even after a "bomber gap," a "missile gap," or a "window of vulnerability" turns out to have been false, there has been no discernible change in defense strategy or in assessment of Soviet goals. Once committed to such a doctrinaire position, the expert without a solid foundation tends to defend it far beyond any reason.

The layman who argues for a nuclear freeze or a nuclear test ban or some other logical arms limitation is frequently put down because he lacks secret information. A prominent weapons advocate, for example, frequently ducks embarrassing questions by saying, "If I could only tell you what I know, you would believe me." That has rarely proved to be the case. There are no secrets on the vital issues that control the future of the human race. Each citizen should realize that his or her judgments are as good as those of the president or the secretary of defense — perhaps even better, since he or she is not subjected to all of the confusing arguments and pressures that impinge on people in official positions.

It is important for the citizen to realize that the government has no monopoly of wisdom or special knowledge that changes the commonsense conclusion that there is "no place to hide." The arms race can only be stopped by an aroused citizenry, confident in its views and prepared to challenge the many myths and misconceptions about nuclear war that have served to prevent exploration of the many safer alternatives. Human beings have no business hiding like rats in a bomb cellar. We have better work to do.

June 1983   Jerome B. Wiesner
                   Massachusetts Institute of Technology

PROLOGUE

NOT SO LONG AGO San Francisco welcomed home the *Independence*, the first of the main target vessels to return from the atom bomb tests at Bikini. Photographs showed the familiar lines of the wrecked ship — her island carried away, her flight deck ripped up, her hangar deck caved in. In the pictures she looked less like a ship than a paper bag blown up and burst. It was the *Independence* all right, exactly as we had left her over a year ago in Kwajalein Harbor.

Anyone who has known a modern carrier in action would be shocked by her mutilation. Although the first shot burst at some distance from her broadside, she was left little more than a derelict. Yet what is more impressive, and likely to be overlooked, is that she remains an outcast ship. The disease of radioactivity lingers on her decks and sides and along her dingy corridors. Blasted first from the air, she survived; smothered later under tons of water, she rode out the tidal wave of the second shot and remained afloat. But the invisible poison of radioactivity she could not throw off. Because of this, not because of structural damage, she had to be towed from Kwajalein home.

She was anchored offshore on strict isolation, a leper. As the papers said: "Newsmen and the public will not be allowed to approach the *Independence*. It is best the Navy believes to view this awful symbol of a possible future from a San Francisco hillside."

Against this whole philosophy the author rebels. Newsmen and particularly the public are just exactly the ones who most need to go aboard and get acquainted with their *Independence!* Ignorance of the law is no excuse in civil courts; just so before the tribunal of all humanity, which now sits in the light and dark corners of the world, ignorance of the natural laws which govern atomic energy cannot be condoned.

The Bikini tests have never received much attention. The accounts of the actual explosions, however well intended, were liberally seasoned with fantasy and superstition, and the results of the tests have remained buried in the vaults of military security.

That sort of security is itself a superstition, and a dangerous one. It fosters misconceptions or, what is worse, indifference, and ultimately results in procrastination, half-measures, and hysteria. There is nothing particularly difficult or mysterious about the scientific principles upon which an atomic explosion is based. Students all over the world are verifying them in the laboratory, and applying them to further research. For some reason Americans have found comfort in the phrase "our industrial know-how." This know-how is our

Maginot Line. Surely our days of grace under this magic symbol are running out.

Perhaps it is good then that the carrier *Independence* should return to America like the proddings of a bad conscience. What happened at Crossroads cannot be buried with the ships in Bikini lagoon or towed away to rot on the beaches of Kwajalein. What happened at Crossroads was the clearest measure yet of the menace of atomic energy. Less spectacular perhaps than Hiroshima and Nagasaki, the Bikini tests give a far clearer warning of the lingering and insidious nature of the radioactive agent which makes it such an ideal weapon for use on civil populations. In the three years of the "atomic era," five bombs (or is it six?) have been exploded. On only these last two or three have men been prepared to study and record the findings under anything like controlled conditions.

What was learned at Bikini of a scientific or military nature may have been of value. Unfortunately much of it is disguised in the esoteric idiom of the scientist. The really great lessons of that experiment, however, belong to no special group but to all mankind. The atomic era, fortunately or otherwise, is now man's environment, to control or to adapt himself to as he can.

Sooner or later "the public" will have to leave their exposed positions on that San Francisco hillside and either retire into caves or come down and take over their *Independence*. For their own protection they will have to match natural laws with civil laws. Science and sociology are as inseparable now as man and his shadow.

No Place to Hide is the Log of a doctor who was assigned to duty with Operation Crossroads. He had reported for duty with the Army in July, 1945, six weeks before Hiroshima, and the following January he joined a score of medical officers to train for the special job of "Radiological Monitors" at the Bikini tests. He learned how to operate a Geiger counter and other instruments important in radiological research. He saw at first hand various installations of the Manhattan District. As a doctor, he concentrated on the dangers of unseen radiation to living tissue and especially to human beings. For the benefit of laymen like himself, he includes at the end of this Log a brief "Guide to the Dangers of Radioactivity."

The first of the Bikini tests took place on July 1, 1946, a date set by President Truman. At least eight months of planning and preparation preceded that event. In that time Joint Task Force One grew from an original few thousand people to something over 40,000, and all plans underwent complete metamorphosis several times. What started as a simple laboratory experiment, to determine the effectiveness of the Bomb used above and under water, became the most complex and intricate project imaginable.

The Navy wanted to test its ships. Ultimately the

target fleet came to include a sample of almost everything that floats: American ships, German ships, Japanese ships, flattops, submarines, battleships, cruisers, destroyers, landing craft, ships made of riveted plates, ships made of welded plates, floating dry docks made of reinforced cement, even seaplanes, were included.

The Army and Navy Air Forces were to be there; the Army, in charge of dropping the first Bomb, began weeks of practice to select its best bomb crew. Both services developed complex plans for guiding pilotless "drone" planes into and through the cloud in order to test stresses and to sample the inner secrets of the dangerous plume.

Scientists of every calling were to be there: marine biologists to study the effect of the Bomb and its radioactive by-products upon the fish and plant life of the islands; oceanographers to study the geology of coral reefs as it might be revealed in the transmission of shock waves following the blast; photographers to take serial pictures of the plume and the waves; physicists and chemists engrossed in their many mysterious pursuits.

Political observers were to be there. With characteristic forthrightness Americans opened the doors to observers from most of the major nations of the world. Newspapermen and photographers found berths available for them. The animal kingdom, too, was represented aboard the ship *Burleson* — not just two of every kind, but hundreds of experimental animals to be tested for the effects of the blast and radioactivity by the Naval Medical Research group.

The men of the Radiological Safety Section, in the colloquialism of the task force, were the "Geiger men." As a sort of Department of Public Health, the Radiological Safety Section included doctors, radiologists, physicists, instruments experts, and almost anyone with a smattering knowledge of electronics. Prepared for the worst, they even had psychiatrists. Concurrently with the task force, they grew from a few score of men to several hundred and eventually were given the use of one of the latest hospital ships of the Navy, the U.S.S. *Haven*, a beautiful white tall-sided ship equipped with ample laboratories, and completely air-conditioned. This last luxury was not so much a concession to the comfort of the scientists as a necessary protection for the delicate electronic instruments used in the detection of radioactivity.

The mission of the Radiological Safety Section in Operation Crossroads may be simply stated in the words of President Truman, who requested Admiral Blandy to take all necessary precautions to see "that no one gets hurt" at Bikini. Men of the Radiological Safety Section were therefore present at most of the activities of the task force. In the air, on the sea, and on board ship, their job was the same, namely to stand guard with Geiger counters for invisible danger from radioactivity. Their assignment began at Bikini, but from there spread to include the neighboring atolls, the hundreds of miles to Eniwetok, Guam, the Philippines, Hawaii, and ultimately to the seaports of the West Coast. Their job, handed on through generations of radiologic monitors, is still going on. Thus the men of the Radiological Safety Section had an unparalleled opportunity to meet the Bomb at close quarters, and to learn something of the public health problem of fissionable materials.

No Log could presume to give the complete picture. But many of the situations encountered at Bikini on Able Day and Baker Day and after are exactly those which civilian and military people alike must face as part of the Cost which they will pay in advance for the promised blessings of atomic energy. They are exactly the problems which enthusiasts for the atomic age are most eager to forget. Initial down payments were made at Hiroshima and Nagasaki. Bikini too is not merely a ravaged and useless little atoll in the deep far Pacific. Bikini is our world.

This Log is not a military document. Neither is it a scientific report. Much of the information the author acquired must remain veiled in official secrecy. This is simply the day-to-day record of a doctor who found himself in the ring with the Bomb and who escaped some of its deadly punches.

The author has emerged with the firm conviction that if life as we know it is to continue, men must understand and deal with the menacing aspects of atomic energy.

Like others trained in the objective and impersonal ways of scientific thought, he had subscribed to the old maxim, "Ye shall know the truth, and the truth shall make you free." But now our new-found knowledge of nuclear energy threatens to enslave or destroy us even before we can understand it fully or learn to use it well. If a Log like this helps to give some inkling of what atomic energy means to the average man, then perhaps the scientific and military facts uncovered at Bikini will have been worth their great cost.

D. B.

1948

No Place to Hide

1946/1984

DEPARTURE

Wednesday, May 29, 1946

For us Operation Crossroads began officially at San Francisco on a glorious morning.

At 9:00 A.M., almost on the minute, two diesel tugs arrived and began the laborious process of turning the U.S.S. *Haven* around. Lines were slacked and dropped in the widening slick of oily water and the few wives who came to see us off began to grow small and inaudible, as we sidled away from the pier. That was our send-off.

A troopship was just coming in, looking dirty and bedraggled, much in need of paint. The decks were lined with figures in khaki who watched us without animation or comment save for an occasional "You'll be sorry," barely audible above the singing of the wind.

Letterman Hospital, the big bridge, Legion of Honor, finally the Cliff House, slipped by. The coast line to the south, that marvelous stretch of beach, was lost in the white turmoil of the breakers, and the white city of

San Francisco, sprawling over the sand to the foot of the hills, was obscured by the spume.

After about an hour out, the ship heaved to while a motor-driven schooner dropped a skiff alongside for the pilot. He plunked neatly into the stern and was rowed out to the pitching schooner without a wave or backward glance. Soon after, our convoy of gulls turned back to the more generous harbor, and now we are officially on our own. Next stop: Pearl Harbor. After that, Bikini and our rendezvous with the task force, and the unknown Bomb.

Thursday, May 30

We are several hundred miles southwest of San Francisco. The ocean is less violent, and has changed perceptibly from the chilling white and slate of the California coast line towards the blue of the tropical Pacific. There is other evidence of the tropics, too. This morning the surface was scattered over with tiny floating jellyfish, or baby man-o'-wars. Delicate, diaphanous creatures, they look like blown cherry blossoms on the windy lawn of the Pacific.

The U.S.S. *Haven* is a good ship, and considering the amount of superstructure she has, she does remarkably little rolling. She is 520 feet long, 70 abeam, and is powered by steam turbines which drive her along at 16 knots. The engines and stack are aft, on the fantail, and so we get little of the vibration and oily smoke.

Saturday, June 1

The "passengers" aboard — Army, Navy, and civilian — number several hundred. Most are older men, some are well-known scientists. Some have worked with radiation in the Manhattan District, but the majority come with little more than a scientific background. Test Able is only one month away. Since this group is to have the responsibility for protecting task force personnel from the invisible dangers of radioactivity, the problem of briefing them on the fundamentals and the practical aspects of radiation is acute.

Today we had our first lectures, up on the balmy navigation deck. It was a session on security. The naval equivalent of a Trial Judge Advocate read us the riot act on security, backing it up with selections from the Federal Espionage Act. Before he got through it began to look as though Bikini would be but a brief stop on the way to Leavenworth. By the nature of our work almost everything we know is potentially dangerous. The law is so general, and the ramifications of radiological safety so widespread, that almost anyone who carries a slide rule is suspect. Actually, of course, there will never be any great control of ideas concerned with atomic energy. The principles have already spread like an epidemic and knowledge of their application is subject only to time. Those of us who have thrown our notebooks over the side today (and one man, his camera) are acting more from superstition than common sense. Nevertheless mine is in Davy Jones's library tonight.

Sunday, June 2

First tropical day. We awoke poorly rested and mothy in our hot cocoon. Air conditioning so far has been a myth. The fresh breeze of yesterday has let go, leaving the ocean hot, glassy, and humid.

The sun is unbelievably potent; even the tanned skins have burned, and everywhere scientific ingenuity stored up in bald pates is blossoming forth with queer turbans and paper nose shields — and always too late. Even the old and wise, it seems, never learn, or at least never remember. They doze a moment in the sun and wake up on fire.

Wednesday, June 5

No Log for our day in Oahu. Hawaii is a gem to be seen, after which it will sparkle in the memory forever. Frank Larson, Tom Madden, and I spent the evening on the beach, a quarter moon overhead, listening to the ebb and flow of home-thoughts in the surf, and wondering what the full of the moon would bring for us in Bikini.

Thursday, June 6

Lectures in theoretical physics have given way to the practical business of the detection of radioactivity. We have been issued an assortment of instruments with which to become familiar. The sun-scorched decks of the *Haven* are alive with schools of monitors moving to and fro in front of pigs of lead in which minute but potent sources of radiation are housed. The picture of a man stooped intently over his small magic box, listening, by means of his earphones, to the incoming barrage of clicks picked up by the Geiger counters is becoming a familiar one.

From the opening in one end of the lead pigs comes a stream of radioactivity as sharp and definite as water from a fire hose. Since it comes from a known source, and dies away as the square of the distance from that source, it is possible to test and calibrate the instruments with fair accuracy. Once this simple task is done, and the principles understood, the monitor has only to make the procedure of interpreting the readings in terms of tolerances and dangers second nature to him. The Geiger counter becomes the sixth sense, a prerequisite to survival in an atomic age.

The Geiger-Müller counter has one big disadvantage: it is too sensitive for the practical kind of work we shall have at Bikini. Designed for detecting radiations almost before there are any present, the G–M counters are jammed and rendered completely useless in the presence of radiation of sufficient intensity to be significant or possibly dangerous. Most of us will entrust our safety to a machine known as an ionization chamber. This type of radiation meter is a thousand times less sensitive than a G–M counter, and was designed for the Normandy invasion, against the possibility of radiation warfare by the Germans.

Such is the nature of our studies, conducted on the skillet of the navigation deck. There are compensations. Evening comes as a great relief and rejuvenation. Sunsets are brief, but prodigal with their color — and then the birth of a nearly full moon. The ship's company gathers on the nav deck for the latest murder mystery film, after which poker games and coffee drinking are resumed in the wardrooms. Venus lights our path to the westward during the evening, and the moon stands the midwatch after midnight. Lights are out on deck, and the ship rolls along in the darkness, following down the silver path toward the ever receding horizon. No hurry, but sure on the course. The great foaming waves build up on the prow; we cut them through and shake them off easily, and new ones come, crash on the side, and drop off into the darkness.

These are pleasant hours, full of inexpressible feelings which mingle and pass like the soft breezes and strange sounds of a Pacific night.

Tuesday, June 11

Tomorrow Bikini! Time has become short. The Commander of Joint Task Force One has less than three weeks to brief and drill his team in the intricate plans for Able Day. The Radiological Safety program is but a small part of the schedule, which calls for the co-ordination of Army bombing, air and ground photography, television, drone air and surface testing (pilotless craft guided by remote control), oceanography, marine biology, press, and so forth.

It will be difficult to convince people of the dangers of radiation, dangers which are evident only upon the dial of some "Geiger machine," especially when you consider what minute amounts of radioactive materials are significant.

Take radium as an example. A few millionths of a gram of radium lodged within the bones of a human may be fatal, as proved years ago by radium dial workers. The material of which the Bomb is made — plutonium — has much the same action and is even more toxic. Once absorbed into the body — via cuts, or breathing, or by eating — these substances are hard to remove. They tend to be deposited in the bones where they either wreck the blood-producing marrow so that the person dies from lack of blood, or they stimulate the formation of fatal bone tumors.

Radiation from the outside — either gamma rays or neutrons — acts to injure or to destroy the cells by ionizing their constituent molecules, much as X rays do. We are accustomed in medicine to using X rays to burn out cancer cells. We know, therefore, about what is safe and what is not. X-ray specialists in this country have set as their safe maximum dose 1/10 of a unit of radiation (the roentgen) per day. This is conservative. A person might be able to take a hundred or a thousand times this amount in a single dose and suffer no permanent effects. Nevertheless, the task force has accepted the standard 0.1 roentgen per day as the maximum allowable daily dose of radiation.

The danger from radiation, like the danger from sunburn, snake poison, strychnine, or almost any other hazard, is merely one of degree. Life on this planet is well accustomed to a measurable amount of radiation. Cosmic rays and the radioactive materials present at the earth's surface total about one roentgen per year, or about 1/36 of the accepted maximum daily tolerance.

But in dealing with the enormous amounts of radiation which will result from the explosion of one atomic bomb, this factor of 36 does not seem like much of a margin of safety. For example, if one ten-millionths of a gram of radium deposited within the body is the maximum amount one may have with reasonable safety, 36 times this, or 36 ten-millionths of a gram, would almost certainly be fatal.

Millionths of a gram would be almost invisible fractions of a grain of table salt. Yet at Bikini we shall not be dealing in grains, nor shovelfuls. It is predicted that the radiation to be born in the Bikini explosions will be the equivalent of *tons* of radium. That is the problem.

Tomorrow, Bikini. Today one of our sleek new destroyers materialized out of the barren ocean, a handsome gray craft, lean, fast, deadly looking. She came prowling up, looked us over well, sniffing around like a giant shark, then settled down to escort us on a parallel course off the starboard quarter. Running at half speed, she was still unraveling a destroyer's beautiful skein of green and white astern. Tonight only her red running light is there to represent the determined power of the U. S. Navy. And in the wardrooms the poker games are wild, stakes are high, tempers reckless.

Wednesday, June 12

Out of a hot sea, out of the hot monotony of an empty Pacific, came a low bright yellow line, and back of it loomed the gray silhouettes of ships. Bikini. A little eggshell of coral, like hundreds of others out here; hitherto unknown, unremembered for glamour or sorrow, it now suddenly becomes a pinpoint in the sea of human affairs, truly a crossroads.

Soon we could make out the contours of the land, with its dense thatch of palms, its steel towers and cluster of dwellings. On either side the land sinks into the breakers emerging further on in little islets or mere sandspits. These frail island excrescences are protected from complete obliteration by a breakwater of red coral — the barrier reef — which surrounds the atoll on its ocean side like a broken picket fence.

The atoll is roughly rectangular, ten miles wide and running twenty to the westward. To the southeast is the "pass," and the main island of Bikini makes up the northeast corner. A hundred and seventy-five miles due west is Eniwetok, and about the same distance southeast is Kwajalein. This is our laboratory.

Rounding in through the pass we entered the quiet turquoise waters of the lagoon to find the fleet packed stern to bow in the anchorage. The target ships are all here, moored in their final array, stiff and solemn as though presenting arms before their last retreat.

The target fleet is composed largely of obsolete ships, some well known and loved. The stanch and storied *Saratoga* is here, third of our big carriers, repeatedly wounded in the past war but still the queen of the fleet. She lies a little apart down toward the pass, and as we crossed close under her bow we could see the assortment of military gear, planes, tanks, and so on, anchored on her flight deck for the test.

The center of the target area is jammed like Gloucester Harbor in a blow: the *New York*, battlewagon of 1912, looking odd, squat, and junky compared to modern ships; the *Pennsylvania;* the *Arkansas* and two old cruisers, the *Pensacola* and the *Salt Lake City*. Strangest of all is the giant Jap battleship, the *Nagato,* an ugly anthropoid creation easily distinguishable by the fantastic fire-control tower. This many-storied, buttressed pile of junk looks as though it had been thrown together without plan or purpose out of odds and ends of American scrap iron.

Dead center in the target is the *Nevada*. She is still a handsome battlewagon. Something about her gracefully pyramiding superstructure appears designed for beauty first and utility second, although those who felt the weight of her mighty guns backing them up at Iwo Jima and Normandy might disagree. She is painted all red now as a better target, and is a ship of singular beauty.

As for the chinks in this target array, they are calked with destroyers, subs, attack transports, landing craft, cement dry docks, and a sample of almost everything in the Navy supply catalogue. Most are naval heirlooms now. Among the modern ships are the light carrier *Independence* and the graceful German battle cruiser *Prinz Eugen*.

This is, of course, a dead fleet, and something of the mute sadness and mystery of the cemetery hangs about the ships as they nose patiently into the trade winds and await their final ordeal. Around the periphery, and up toward the main island of Bikini, is anchored the live fleet in all its gay regalia, colors flying, signals blinking, small boats churning the lagoon into streaks of foam. Who knows? Perhaps this live fleet, for all its vain vitality, is also out of date — like ourselves, not designed for atomic wars.

Thursday, June 13

A task force of this size is an enormously complex organism. The problem at Bikini is not a direct objective

— the taking of a beachhead, or a hit-run attack on an enemy naval base. It is not simply a matter of lining up the ships, blasting them, and recording the results. At least seven distinct groups of interests coalesce in Joint Task Force One, each with its plans and requirements worked out in great detail. They are:

(1) The Navy, which is responsible for the over-all arrangement and care of ships, the control of damage (as far as will be possible), the recording of results, and the ultimate disposal of what remains of the target fleet.

(2) The Naval Air Force, flying out of islands and off flattops, which will be engaged in numerous photographic projects, and the problem of flying pilotless ships through the "cloud" on very secret scientific missions.

(3) The Army, which will participate in many quarters, and especially in the Radiological Safety Section.

(4) The Army Air Force, basing its fleet of B–29's on Kwajalein, whose job it is to deliver the little Bomb to the right place at the right time. A more potent package was never opened on this earth, and one can only pray that, as with Pandora's box, when the contents are revealed, hope may still remain with us.

(5) Science, too, is interested. Besides both Services, hundreds of civilian specialists are involved in most elaborate experiments. They

include the study of the composition of the
cloud, the intensity of the blast wave, and
the intensity and kind of radiation produced
during the blast, for which a great variety of
instruments are to be stationed aboard ships,
and on the surrounding islets; the study of the
effects of blast and radioactivity on experimental animals, for which the Naval Medical Research Bureau has assigned an entire ship, complete with animals and M.D.'s; the study of the
effects of radioactivity on the fish and plant
population; the effect, if any, of the blast upon
the structure of a coral atoll; and the dissemination of radioactive materials by currents of air
and water. These are but a few of the projects
proposed by scientific minds.

Somewhere in that intermediate zone which
combines both science and humanism, as always, comes medicine, whose chief interest, as
expressed in the Radiological Safety Section,
is in protecting the task force from dangerous
radiation. It is the new and almost unexplored
problem of public health in the atomic age.

(6) Politics, too, is interested in Bikini. Observers
from Washington, and from many nations,
some of them already with us on the U.S.S.
Haven, will be on hand to get their kinder-
garten course in atomic energy.

(7) And the press, with its regiment of photographers and cargo ships of flash bulbs. They

will be with us, on the ships and in numerous special photographic planes. Someone has said that half of the world's supply of photographic film will be on hand for the two tests. If that were true, and if half of the world's opinion might thereby be influenced, the investment would well be worth while.

Perhaps in the long run the most important people out here are the politicians, the foreign representatives, and the newsmen. Perhaps one should not categorize at all. Operation Crossroads is not an experiment undertaken by Army, Navy, and civilian specialists. It is not even an American project, to which have been invited foreign representatives. It is a test conducted by many different people, and a world of men, women, and their children will participate in its results.

This, in rough outline, is the make-up of Joint Task Force One. The prospect of co-ordinating the activities of two Armed Services, two Air Forces, the strict requirements of scientific investigation, and the demands of political and journalistic observers would seem to be a hopeless one. At the moment they seem to add up to sheer confusion on a logarithmic scale. Nevertheless, they must all ultimately dovetail perfectly and come to a sharp focus on the split second referred to as "How Hour" in the plans for Able and Baker Days.

Some of this confusion Frank Larson and I were able to see today at first hand aboard the control ship. A communications ship by design, this vessel is to be the nerve center of the task force. On the test days all information regarding the location and intensity of damage and radiation will be radioed directly to the control room, and from there, with that information, the activities of the entire fleet can be co-ordinated. But today with the detailed plans of each airplane and each small boat unit being worked out, and with an air rehearsal going on overhead, this particular nerve center seemed to be having an epileptic seizure.

Lars and I have been assigned to the Naval Air Group, based near Kwajalein, whose duty it will be to make low altitude reconnaissance over the lagoon and target fleet immediately after the first explosion. Whatever hazards that may involve, we are thankful not to be having a desk job aboard the control ship when things start getting hot.

Unable to get any information about our assignment, we returned to the *Haven* and learned that we were to report to a Navy Captain in charge of all ships' damage control who would be flying with one of us on Able Day. We hitched a ride over to his ship, and had an interesting interview with him. Tall, angular, florid, and completely bald, the Captain gives the impression of one who likes his authority but takes it easily. We were amazed to find how well briefed in the practical side of radiation he is.

After the interview he offered us his private skimmer

for our return, and went to the gangway to see that we
got it. On the quarter-deck there was quite a commotion.
Side Boys in white were everywhere. This, as we were
to learn, was not for us; as we started down the gang-
plank, the Officer of the Deck shouted: "Hey, soldier,
you can't go down there. Orders to keep it clear."

"Well, how do we get off this bucket?"

"You'll have to go forward and use the other gangway."

The Captain then very kindly offered to pilot us. And
as we crept forward through the dark passage we could
hear him muttering, half to us, "What do they get so
damned stewed up about when some brass is coming
aboard? What the hell, you'd think it was MacArthur."

Friday, June 14

Today we had our final briefing from Colonel Staf-
ford Warren, chief of the Radiological Safety Section.
The plan for Able Day is a fascinating one, involving
the movements of thousands of people in hundreds of
widely separated units, whose second hands must con-
verge together on the final How Hour.

The plan is roughly this:

Weather permitting, Test Able will be held, according to the President's direction, on July 1. The Bomb
will be dropped from a B–29 at an unspecified altitude
and radio silence from all air and surface craft at this
time will enable everyone in the task force to hear the

bombardier's broadcast of their bomb run and final release. The live fleet will be coasting along twenty to thirty miles upwind, while in the air, and at varying distances, will be numerous planes, flying photographic, radiological reconnaissance, and numerous other missions. All personnel will be required to wear specially designed, extremely dense goggles, for in the first few millionths of a second of the actual explosion a tremendous flash of ultraviolet radiation is released.

It is hard to convince the mind of the magnitude of this explosion. We are told, for example, that the power of the Bomb is the equivalent of 20,000 tons of T.N.T. But who of us has ever seen a Hercules Powder Plant go up, or even a small wheelbarrow full of T.N.T. blow? We are told that the intensity of the heat and flash at the instant of detonation will be equal to that of the sun. The ball of fire which then envelops the target center, representing the heat generated by the explosion, is about half a mile in diameter. As it expands, it rises, becoming a sphere, wrapped in smoke and steam, and at last collapses into a tremendous uprushing convection current, climbing at the rate of about 10,000 feet a minute to the stratosphere.

Of course no planes will be allowed in the vicinity of the cloud. The intensity of radiation present in that boiling column of vapors would certainly be lethal to personnel, even if the plane could survive the physical beating. Instead, however, the pilotless airplanes are to be flown into and through the cloud at different levels.

After the cloud has been carried away by the trade winds, the first cautious probings into the target area will be made by two Navy flying boats — Martin PBM–5's — which will make sweeps over the area at progressively lower altitudes until dangerous radiation is encountered.

This interesting little reconnaissance job has fallen to Lars and me. Our planes are to be equipped with a variety of instruments so that radiation of several kinds and intensities may be picked up. According to our findings, radioed in to the control ship, and from information from automatic self-broadcasting Geiger counters located on buoys within the target area, the subsequent plan of attack by the task force can be directed. Small surface craft, and eventually landing parties, will be sent in. What they will find and what they will have to do cannot be predicted, but they will have to keep a constant close check on the lagoon water, and if possible attempt to beach any sinking or burning vessels.

In the steady trade winds, the giant plume may be expected to hold together for some time. Army airplanes and Navy destroyers will ride hard on the outlaw as far as they can follow it, and Eniwetok, 175 miles roughly downwind, may have to be unceremoniously evacuated.

Such is the plan for Able Day, as described by the Colonel in our final briefing today. We drew our instruments and gear; tomorrow the air contingent moves to

Kwajalein. Lars, Tom, Charlie Wells and several others of us make up a smaller group who will be based on Ebeye, next to Kwaj, where the Navy has its seaplane squadrons.

This afternoon after getting our assignments and our gear most of us went ashore to drink beer and think it over. The sun was rich with its tropical intensity, and the sky full of the clustering thunderheads. The beauty of this Bikini setting seems to belong to another world entirely, having no relation to the strange mission which brings us here.

From a small boat one really gets an idea of the size of a task force. Ships are everywhere, standing up stark and stolid and black against the cathedral clouds, their tall sides richly stained with rust. The shoaling water, full of dispersed coral, is luminous, and the breezy surface flashes like an ice floe of mirrors.

The main island of Bikini is a crescent of sand, four miles long and a couple of hundred yards wide. Though untouched by war, it has been pretty well ravaged in the preparations for these tests. Floating dry docks and broken-up landing craft line its beautiful sweep of sand; numerous towers have been erected for fixed photographic and television instruments; and the Seabee detachments and the two recreation areas have pretty well disposed of the rest of the island. The dispossessed Bikini natives, of course, have long since been removed to another atoll, and even discounting the possibility of lingering radioactivity it is doubtful if this island could support them again for a generation.

The officers' club was doing a land-office business in dispensing cold drinks, and after a couple, just to make up for the day's dehydration, Tom and Lars and I got to brooding over our assignment. Our main worry concerned the possibility of finding the air over the lagoon full of dangerous radioactive particles. We had been issued gas masks, the ordinary assault masks, but no one seemed to know whether or not they would filter out fission products. The B–29's will be all right, since they have cabins which can be sealed off and pressurized with oxygen. But not the old flying boats which were not designed for high altitude flying.

So we looked up our old friend Dr. Hirschfelder, of Wisconsin. He is what is officially known as a "Phenomenologist." On hearing our problem, he proceeded to make a few logarithmic calculations on the back of an envelope, then announced that the dispersion of the fission products would be so great as to constitute no hazard. "Oh, no. You would all be dead from radiation before you could inhale enough to hurt you."

That was comforting, but we pressed the point: "So you think that the gas masks are superfluous?"

"Yes, I do."

"And if you ran into a cloud of hot stuff, you would not bother to wear one?"

"I, well — " putting the envelope back in his coat

pocket — "Yes. Yes, I probably would, though I couldn't tell you why."

Saturday, June 15

On to Ebeye. The flight down to Kwajalein gave us our first relief impression of coral atolls. Seen from above, the delicate irregular chains of islets and sand bars are so many necklaces of tiny green and yellow jewels, strung on a frayed silken strand of surf. Oceanwards one usually sees a shallow tidewater shelf running out sometimes as much as half a mile and bounded by the jagged red-brown barrier reef and its concentric pattern of combers. From here out the atoll drops precipitously away into the cobalt of deep water. Lagoonwards the water deepens more gradually, and passes through a spectrum of greens and blues of marvelous intensity. Submerged pillars of coral — coral heads, they are called — show up as brown and olive islands against the brilliant turquoise of the sandy bottom.

Our course was southeast 175 miles to the main island of the Kwajalein Atoll. Ebeye lies just four miles north, and both are at the southeast corner of the atoll. Heavy fighting took place on both islands, and along the way one sees a number of rusting hulks of Jap ships beached inside the lagoon, chin-up on the reef and sterns in deep water.

Once over our tiny island of Ebeye, with all its minia-ture houses, and the harbor with its toy ships, we came down in a mad plunge, leveled off just above the choppy waves, skimmed in between lanes of great vessels, and finally settled into a smother of foam. Up at the cement launching ramp Marshallese natives swam out to hook on the enormous rubber wheels, two forward and one aft. Then tail first we were hauled up onto the apron. So we arrived at Ebeye — treeless Ebeye — one mile long and 150 yards wide — and reported for duty.

Monday, June 17

Ebeye was a seaplane base for the Japanese before us. The L-shaped wharf, cement apron, and landing ramp were constructed by them. These, together with a few grass-grown trenches and an old brackish well, are all that are left to indicate the former tenure. Instead one sees Quonset huts and barracks, repair sheds and nose hangars, a chapel, a baseball field, an outdoor movie pavilion, a shore line of half-buried junk, and a sky line of rusting oil drums — these are the trademarks of American occupancy.

One single stubborn pandanus tree still survives — a stark determined scarecrow of a tree — standing beside the officers' club. Near by are the skipper's house and the guest house where traveling USO shows stay, and in the shallows in front, a fair-sized swimming pool has been blasted out of the flinty coral.

Not far up the beach from the skipper's house is our Quonset hut, an airy structure without doors or windows. This has some advantages. Squalls of rain come sweeping over at intervals throughout the day and night, and while there is nothing to keep the horizontal rain out, neither is there anything to keep it in.

We are on the windward and seaward shore. A fresh breeze is constantly blowing, salty, invigorating, and full of the thunder of the near-by surf. At full tide the onrushing waves reach almost to our doorstep.

This afternoon, Commander Pew, skipper of our seaplane squadron, called a meeting of all hands in the briefing room. Tomorrow is to be a rehearsal of all air groups, and in less than a week the final dress rehearsal takes place. The men of this squadron are good American types, clean-cut, vigorous, grimy, gum-chewing characters dressed in shorts and sandals cut from GI boots. Morale is clearly no problem on Ebeye. All they wanted from us Geiger men was an assurance of continuing manhood, and they would be willing to tackle an atomic bomb every morning before breakfast, if not before coffee.

Lars is to fly with Commander Pew, who will also have the Navy damage-control expert whom we met in Bikini. I will fly with Lieutenant Lower. Tom and Charlie are to stand by with the rescue ships, and the rest of our group will be in photographic missions.

Down on the apron the giant flying boats are being readied for tomorrow's flight. One by one their engines sputter and roar into earth-shaking life. One by one the ships are being trundled down to the launching ramp, and then taxied out to moorings in the lagoon. Flights begin at dawn.

Tuesday, June 18

Spot time was set at 4:30. We arose an hour early to find the darkness crying with wind and the promise of rain. There is something about an approaching storm which gives warning though it cannot be seen: there is a new undertone to the surf, a sound not exactly ominous, but deep and persistent; the wind seems more restless and the darkness more black. But for us there was nothing to do but climb into sticky clothing and stumble to the wharf. Shortly before take-off time word came of storms at Bikini and official postponement of the rehearsal. So we returned to our sacks to doze and watch the dawn come up, gray, misty, full of rain squalls.

Tom, Lars, and I, having nothing better to do, caught the midmorning boat to Kwajalein, to have a look around, and buy something just for the feel of buying something again. Kwajalein is no longer a romantic South Sea isle. It is a boom town gone bust, temporarily sustained by the Bikini tests. Mud, barracks, Quonset huts, hangars, barbed wire, and more mud. Around the hangars, and the landings, around the swimming beach and the officers' clubs, there is activity; elsewhere disuse and rapid decay.

There is still considerable evidence of the battle of

Kwajalein. A shattered concrete pillbox stands like a monument on the main wharf. There are almost no trees. The beaches are tidewater junk yards strewn with the wreckage of landing craft and half-buried machinery. The patient labors of sand and storm and rust will clear away the wreckage, but Kwaj has finished its history as a lovely tropical isle.

Kwaj, too, is crescentic in shape; fortunately its longest limb is roughly parallel to the trade winds, so that a landing strip ample for the big planes could be made. Thus the island will remain one of many tiny links in the illusion of national defense.

The Kwajalein contingent will be flying in B–29's on cloud-tracking, photography, and various observation missions. The Radiological Safety group over there has fared even worse with their instruments than we have. The humid and salt-laden atmosphere has already shorted out more than half of their Geiger counters.

We went down to the airstrip, which occupies two thirds of the island. At one end of that mile-long strip of macadam, the B–29's and giant cargo ships are lined up at parade rest. Those concerned with Operation Crossroads are under armed guard. The photographic planes can be identified by the black "P" on an orange field, painted on their rudders. Others bear an emblem of black chain lightning, indicating that they are detailed to pick up and measure the shock wave of the first atomic blast as it is propagated through the air.

Dave's Dream, the already famous drop ship, whose crew has been practicing their bomb run for months, is easily identified by the large black "B" on her fin. She stands entirely apart, on the far side of the runway. There, next to the ocean, and nearly half a mile from the regular installations, a special ramp has been built to facilitate loading of the Bomb. Not far away is a group of Quonset huts and some cement vaults where the national secret and its attending scientists keep their strict isolation. *Dave's Dream*, tail-high on the ramp, looks set for a flying start as soon as the hot stuff comes aboard.

Wednesday, June 19

Up again at 3:45 A.M. So was the storm — a real tropical front — bringing rain in torrents, another postponement of the rehearsal, and sweet oblivion.

Thursday, June 20

Clearing weather. Last night a dispatch came from Bikini, "Prepare to execute," and before dawn the squadron was launched and taxiing around in the lagoon until there was light enough for the take-off.

Dawn in the tropics comes suddenly; like the development of a photograph, suddenly out of the blank nothingness you become aware of vague outlines, and a moment later the shore, the towers, and the lagoon full of ships are all about you.

Receiving radio clearance from Ebeye, one by one our giant birds swung into the wind; gathering speed, with the foam streaming behind like discharging rockets, they lifted themselves from the breezy sea lane, passed noisily over Ebeye, and swung off on a course for Bikini.

These big patrol bombers are perfectly suited to our radiological reconnaissance. The pilot and co-pilot sit well up in the nose, above and behind the nose gunner. Behind them is the navigation deck, with a large navigation table, the radarscope, and the radio, and lastly the ship's engineer station with its banks of instruments. The largest part of my work will be at the navigation table, where there is room for my instruments and the charts and overlays of our flight pattern.

Beneath the navigation deck and cockpit is an ample galley with a good electric stove. We were no sooner well off the water than the rich smell of eggs and bacon eddied through the ship, relaxing the tensions of the take-off and bringing forth a stream of pleasant banter through the interphone. Soon the engineer's assistant appeared with food and coffee, and by the time we were wiping the last grease from our chins our skipper, Lieutenant Lower, was talking with Commander Pew and preparing to let down through the clouds to Bikini.

Clouds were heavy at 6000 feet, but down on the deck there was good visibility, and we found the atoll just ahead. High above us was a great assemblage of aircraft. Most of them we did not see, but we could hear them calling in to the control ship. Somewhere above us, at tremendous altitude, was the drop ship, going through its routine and broadcasting its bombing runs.

Radio discipline is, of course, imperative, and that is a most difficult discipline. There was a joker called "War Paint" who felt lonely. He kept our circuit jammed with plaintive bleatings for someone to chat with. Then there was another character named "Antique One." His radioman must have studied Greek, for he kept calling in: "This is Antigone One, Antigone One — " No one knew who Antigone One was, so, of course, no one answered. But for the most part the communications were satisfactory. We could hear Larson transmitting each leg of the practice run as he completed it: "Leg four, two thousand feet, no radiation found" or "Leg six completed, two thousand feet, background radiation 100 counts per minute." (Ordinarily one will hear about 35 counts per minute, but in a plane there is enough radium in the instrument dials to triple the true background.)

The plan of our lagoon survey had been worked out in great detail. Commander Pew and Larson went in first, about 30 minutes after the first shot when the evil cloud had passed. We followed a few minutes later.

With our trial runs completed, the control ship radioed our clearance for home. Our skipper, however, had one more mission to perform. Coming in over the straggling live fleet he picked out the white hospital ship *Bountiful*. Letting down to masthead height and going into a vertical bank he twice circled the ship. I could see nothing for looking down the barrel of the smokestack, but at last, apparently satisfied, he began straightening out, wagged his wings, and began his climb. Who the girl was no one seemed to know, nor did Lieutenant Lower offer any hint.

A small, alert, weatherbeaten fellow, the skipper obviously loves flying and knows every plate and rivet of his ship from galley to radarscope. His crew he treats with friendly banter, but at the same time nothing ever seems to get by him. You hear him shout over the interphone:

"What's going on back there? Who lit that match?" After an awful silence comes the voice of the engineer: "I did, sir. I'm on the nav deck."

"Okay Carlson."

Or another time: "Hey, back in the waist — who opened that port?"

"I did, sir. This Marine photographer said he had to get some pictures of the fleet — "

"All right, but next time let me know before you open things up. I'm not worried about the Marine — we can get plenty of them — but I've only got one ship." Then as an afterthought: "Did he get any pictures of the *Bountiful?*"

"Yes, sir."

"Tell him he owes me one, will you?"

"Aye, aye, sir."

We flew back in formation. The thunderheads were piled up into great mountain ranges above the stratus clouds. Around their buttresses and down their bottomless canyons our formation found its way, mere insects against the clouds, reveling in that dreamlike unreality of time and place, until Kwajalein began to show on our radar and we were home again.

Saturday, June 22

Bright day, lazy and full of laundry. The lagoon has been the quintessence of blue today; inside the wall of surf the many little islands and the dark ships stand out clear and sharp.

Lars and I busied ourselves constructing an air scoop to conduct air from outside our ships to the instruments on the nav table. This will enable us to test the atmosphere outside for radioactive particles while still having the ships closed up tight. Unlike the B–29's, these PBM–5's are not hermetically sealed, and so we shall have to trust our health to the unknown mercies of our gas masks.

Tomorrow is the final dress rehearsal. Up on the apron the motors are being tuned, the radio gear tested, the fuel tanks filled. It takes a lot of work to put a squadron of giant seabirds into the air.

Sunday, June 23

The "Queen Day" dress rehearsal has been postponed because of cloudy weather. Colonel Talbot, chief of our

Air Reconnaissance Group, dropped in on his way back from Bikini for a swim and a word of caution regarding the care of instruments. Apparently the mortality of the Geiger counters among the main task force from causes human and climatic has become of epidemic proportions.

One of the great and recurring pleasures of Ebeye's simple life is sunset. In this cloud-bound Shangri-La sunsets are spread with all of nature's spendthrift splendor. We were watching the spectrum play its fancy out upon the high crests tonight when out of the dark an F6F (Hellcat) came screaming over the base. He buzzed us a couple of times and radioed down that a Piper Cub carrying two officers had run out of gas and had been forced down in the lagoon. Could a crash boat attempt the rescue? It was believed that they had been able to land on the shore of a tiny island about twenty miles up the chain. The F6F would go along to guide the boat, as visibility was much better from the air.

At that news Ebeye came to life and went roaring in all six of its jeeps down to the landing. I happened to be sitting in one of the jeeps at the time and was swept along with the rest in the general excitement. Down on the wharf the duty crash boat was warming up and slacking its lines when we jumped aboard. By this time inky black night was upon us; nevertheless, our skipper — a fearless, if almost beardless, gum-chewing old sea dog of about nineteen years — opened her to 3/4 throttle and went swirling through the shipping anchored in the lagoon.

A thick fog hung on the water, so that our own search-lights blinded us, and a cold choppy wind was blowing. When you are running at 20 knots in a Stygian fog, knowing the lagoon to be studded with coral heads that lie almost awash, the plywood planking under you seems a little frail. But with God as our co-pilot, and the Hellcat above acting as navigator, we managed the twenty miles without accident.

We did have one close call, running right up to the barrier reef before seeing it. In a matter of seconds, the water turned blue, then jade, then white. A warning message from the jittery buzz-boy above was all that kept us from going hard on for the rest of the night. You could see the line of surf about thirty yards away, and the shadow of our crash boat showed clearly on the white coral immediately below.

After that we followed the F6F more closely and tried no short cuts. It was a rough trip, especially for the two lookouts stationed on the bow. Half of the time they were lost in spray. Silvery flying fish, like mad phantoms, were buzzing out of the waves, lurching in all directions, unable to get their bearings in the unaccustomed light. One of the crew amused himself by firing .45 caliber slugs at them. He got no hits, but his nonchalance kept our courage up.

Finally, the island was located and a faint light flickering on shore identified the lost party. We called for flares from the F6F. He had none. Neither had we. So the skipper circled his craft several times in order to get in as close as possible to the barrier reef. Heaving to, we got one of the rubber boats inflated and out overside. Two sailors clambered gingerly into the squashy raft, set their oars, and pulled away, nodding to the shouted instructions from the skipper. They made poor headway. A stiff wind was blowing abeam of their course, carrying them toward the slough between the islands. Beyond this lay the barrier reef, the surf, and the Pacific.

Sailors can be the most profane and uncouth men on earth, and yet in a crisis they are crazy courageous. It would be impossible to record the language they use. It is so degenerate, so monotonously vile, that even the most blasphemous expressions become meaningless. And yet, without any hesitation, indeed with oaths, gibes, and laughter, the lads shoved off in their flimsy craft. Black night, surf and a reef ahead, whitecaps and a strong quartering wind, sharks and barracuda below — off they went.

The skipper was jittery. Once they cleared our bow it became increasingly evident that they could never paddle back against the wind even if they could make shore. So he drove full ahead, almost resting his bow on the reef, and notwithstanding their protests, snatched them aboard, and backed away. Then he radioed the F6F that the landing was too dangerous to attempt; they would return for the men in the morning. The pilot gave us a "Roger" and explained that he had only fuel for ten minutes longer. He gave us our heading for Ebeye; then his lights rapidly faded into misty stars in the direction of Kwajalein. We were home in an hour, wet and pulpy. As for the "Queen Day" dress rehearsal, the order has come from the command ship: "Prepare to execute."

DRESS REHEARSAL

Monday, June 24, 1946

We executed. Before dawn the B–29's from Kwajalein were rumbling by overhead. We followed as soon as visibility returned to the lagoon and were up among the thunderheads just as their crests began to take the first rosy blush. Dawn in the Himalayas could not have been more beautiful; gigantic white mountains were standing up all about us, pink and motionless, and between them the cloud canyons, the gorges, and precipices were still brimming with night.

At Bikini the weather steadily improved. We passed over the live fleet, strung out in Indian file, gliding along, some twenty miles or more east of Bikini Atoll. There was something savage and premeditated in its silent, watchful progress. Overhead the drop ship was making practice runs over the target about every thirty minutes. We could hear him plainly on the radio. "Ten minutes before first live bomb run." We were flying in tight circles with Commander Pew's ship just ahead. "Beginning first live bomb run. Two minutes before bomb release. Adjust all goggles." We placed them on our foreheads. "One minute before bomb release. All goggles must be adjusted." We waited tensely, all of us shutting ourselves up inside the midnight of those goggles, and the ship being put on automatic pilot. Larson's ship, only two miles ahead, was also flying on instruments.

Then came the word: "Coming up on bomb release. Negative, negative, negative. Target obscured by clouds. Predicted time of next bomb run 30 minutes." Thirty minutes later we again straightened out, set the ships under automatic pilot, and went under the goggles. This time visibility must have been satisfactory, for we heard the words: "Bomb away. Bomb away. Bomb away." Then another long wait before we could remove our goggles. Larson's ship, miraculously, was still ahead, just where it had been before. Of course, this was only a rehearsal; no bomb was dropped.

Commander Pew then took his plane in over the target fleet and Larson began making his measurements. We have found that it will take three men working in close teamwork to make anything like accurate measurements of the radiation on Able Day. One man will have his hands full locating the ship along the predetermined leg by means of a stop watch. The second will prepare the messages to be transmitted at the end of each leg. As for me, I shall have six instruments to read and interpret: two Geiger-Müller counters set to different ranges of sensitivity; two ionization chambers, one set to tolerable and one to dangerous ranges of intensity; one alpha counter connected to the wind scoop for the detection of the highly toxic plutonium in the air; and a proteximeter which will indicate the aggregate dose. This should suffice to give a rough working measure of the radiation. The first indication of radiation will be picked up on the headphones of the Geiger counters. At the other end of the range the ionization chambers will inform us of dangerous levels of radiation. The major deficiency is in the alpha counter. Such an instrument is so delicate as to be thrown off by changes in moisture and temperature, or merely by the breeze from the air scoop. Like the gas masks, we will take them along, and yet not really know why.

The target fleet looked beautiful. From a plane at two thousand feet one gets an excellent view of the ships, standing at parade rest on the placid lagoon. The handsome *Nevada*, formerly entirely red, has been given a trimming of white for better identification. Near her lie the major vessels — the *New York*, the *Arkansas*, the *Pennsylvania;* the cruisers *Salt Lake City* and *Pensacola;* the beautiful *Sara;* the trim light flattop, *Independence;* the hulking black *Nagato;* and down to leeward at some distance the graceful gray *Prinz Eugen.*

Running out from the *Nevada* is a radial pattern of old destroyers and transports. Being more or less of a kind they should give the best indication of the relationship of damage to distance from the bomb.

Considered as an experiment it seems to be a pretty good target array. One major factor, however, remains uncontrolled: the exact center of the explosion. It probably would be better to have the Bomb erected upon the superstructure of the *Nevada*, or placed in a barrage balloon which could be suspended above the fleet at a known fixed point.

Nothing was stirring aboard the ships, or in the lagoon. They lay quietly at anchor. They would be exactly so at H Hour on Able Day, save for the addition of instruments and experimental animals which will be put aboard the evening before the test.

Somehow, looking down upon this silent task force, cozily riding anchor, gently yawing to the mild trade winds and surrounded by a chain of bright islets and the fathomless blue Pacific — somehow it is hard to imagine that they belong to a scientific experiment. Rather they should be serving the cause of art. I would a thousand times rather that Bikini and its tiny ships should remind man of the beauty of his world and of his creative aptitudes, instead of his curiously childish genius for destruction.

Wednesday, June 26

Two days have passed. Between flights life is slow at Ebeye. One perpetual job has to be done, namely the overhauling of our ships, but that does not help to distinguish one day from another. We wake to the booming of the surf, and fall asleep to its steady chant. Between these limits one may take aboard his three squares, swim, collect shells, read, and do laundry. This last item is easier on Ebeye than with a Bendix. You hang your shirt out on a line, and settle back with a book. After the next rain squall has passed, you collect the shirt, now well rinsed of salt, and give it a brief treatment with soap. After that, to the line once more with it and you back to the book. Another squall arrives, rinses out the soap, and departs, leaving the hot sun and breeze to finish the work. Men of distinction can use the ship's laundry, where in a matter of weeks you can get a shirt laundered and pressed, along with the impartial removal of all buttons.

Swimming is our best preoccupation. The lagoon water is comfortably warm; away from the shore it is quite clear, and of course teeming with life. Underwater goggles are the open-sesame to a fascinating new world. Without them you would never suspect what lies beneath the breezy surface. With them, you are at once transported into an enchanted kingdom. Coral growing in the shape of plants and trees, crags and castles, is everywhere seen in multicolored splendor.

There seems to be little hazard in swimming where it is not too deep. The big sharks and octopuses prefer deeper water, and barracuda packs are rarely reported. Giant sea clams are often found on the bottom, their enormous fluted shells open, but the lacework of their

mantles is so strikingly beautiful as never to be overlooked.

Thursday, June 27

One sees little of the Marshallese natives here; most
of them have been removed to islands up the chain. There
are a few boys around, however, making beds for officers, and waiting on table at mess. They are Microne-
sians, smallest of the three native races of the Pacific
islands. They are darker and less handsome than the
Polynesians of Samoa, and have none of the black,
menacing mien of the Melanesians of the Fijis. Those
whom we have come to know are quiet, imperturbable,
honest, and extremely proud. They will have none of the
white-Negro relationship. These are their islands, and
we the strangers. While they are accustomed to subjec-
tion, they seem to have an assurance that the Americans,
like the Japanese and the Germans before them, will one
day pass on and be replaced. So why get excited or
take sides? The only thing to do is get along.

Our native boys speak no language we can understand. Yet they seem to know in a general way our
wishes. If you give them your plate and say slowly and
carefully: "More meat, please," they will nod with apparent understanding, and then return with canned
peaches, or a bottle of Worcestershire sauce, or perhaps
the whole meal starting over from the beginning.

Colonel Talbot, head of our air group, dropped in

today with mail and the latest instructions from the U.S.S. *Haven*. Among other preparations for Able Day, we were instructed to make blood counts on ourselves. I doubt if there is the slightest scientific value in making a single blood count per radiological monitor, but it serves again to illustrate how difficult it is to assess the damage resulting from radiation, and to carry out preventive measures.

The belief that radiation affects the blood has become deep-rooted in people's minds since the days when a number of the radium dial workers, making luminous clocks, died of an acquired anaemia. This concept also has received additional support from stories that people in Hiroshima and Nagasaki have died from anaemia or from hemorrhage.

These things are true. The same situation can be produced in experimental animals by exposing them to X rays. At certain levels of radiation, the animals will die of massive and uncontrollable hemorrhage, usually from the bowels, which are delicate and especially vulnerable. This happens a week or two after a heavy dose of X rays, and appears to be due to the disruption of the normal clotting mechanism.

With lower but repeated doses of radiation, the animals may survive this bleeding phase, only to die in a few months, like the radium dial workers, of a lack of blood resulting from injury to the blood-producing bone marrow.

As with any other toxic agent, the danger of radiation depends upon three factors: (1) the nature or kind of radiation, (2) the dose, and (3) the resistance of the individual. X-ray specialists in this country have agreed that one can probably take a tenth (1/10) of a roentgen every day and not be injured. That is about the amount of radiation a person gets who stands up for an ordinary X ray of his chest. A study for stones in the gall bladder will amount to six or seven roentgens. If you have an ulcer and have to have a study made of the stomach and upper intestinal tract under a fluoroscope you might get anywhere from 10 to 40 roentgens. That probably won't hurt you if you don't have to have it repeated every two weeks. Indeed, given radiation to small areas of the body, in doses such as we often have to give in treating cancer, a person can stand 6000 to 8000 roentgens. However, if the dose is spread over the entire body, several hundred roentgens would probably be lethal.

It is this radiation to the body as a whole which we must expect in working with the atomic bomb. Conceivably one of us could accidentally get himself overdosed with radiation and die as other experimental animals do. We are in the business of creating radiation out here — really fantastic amounts of radiation, estimated by the Colonel as the equivalent of tons of radium.

If so injured by a fatal exposure, doubtless our blood counts would show the expected changes. But to a dead man this is academic. A far more important practical consideration is whether or not blood tests can be used to indicate dangerous but sublethal exposures. Could they, for example, be used to safeguard the health of crews going aboard ships after the shots? Would they indicate when a man is getting too much, and do so in time to get him out of his hazardous assignment? Or, to give the problem wider scope, in the event of an atomic war, would blood tests be of any value in protecting the fire fighters and engineers at work in a bombed city?

That is the hitch. When would there be time for such complex measures? One blood count is meaningless. First you must establish the normal for each individual. To do this accurately would require five or ten blood determinations taken before exposure. After exposure frequent check-ups would be necessary to determine any downhill trend. This meticulous determination of the normal is necessary because exposures of significance to the patient might be reflected in only slight variations in the blood.

Blood tests were made by the thousands in the Manhattan District, where the clean and controllable conditions of a scientific laboratory were available. But during an atomic war there would be no time for such precise measurements. Typical field conditions would exist there and immediate decisions would have to be made based on the crude and practical measurements available.

Thus, it seems doubtful that either science or humanity will be advanced many micra by our making isolated observations on our blood now, a few days before Able Day. The order is understandable. Under the circumstances there is not much else to do. There is no harm in it provided no one is deluded by the false security of such a scientific fetish.

Saturday, June 29

Weather is again perfect. After nearly three weeks of bad weather, we have hit a fair streak. Clouds are white, cottony, and not smudged down with rain. The moon has gone, leaving us surrounded by the black chasm of the Pacific night. The breakers on the reef glow and fade all up and down the length of the island, and the deep insomniac breathing of the ocean is always beside you. Pale terrestrial sand crabs flee from you along the beach and vanish into their holes like vague hallucinations.

Out of the black east a black wind brings the haunting music of Cape Cod in other summers, night cruises in the phosphorescent seas of late August, the desolate gonging of the bell buoys and faraway foghorns, the flutter of the sails. Strange how it can be all around you — your life — nearer and clearer than the breakers on the reef and yet no more retrievable than the lonely passing wind.

Sunday, June 30

Final preparations for all hands. The crews have been swarming over their planes for days, and now their old and overworked engines are tuned to the last horse-power. All day they have been coughing, sputtering, roaring, sending clouds of sand across the ramp, and whipping the water into hurricane spume along the shore.

The planes themselves have had to be cleaned from stem to tail gunner with gasoline so that there will be no greasy spots to collect radioactive particles from the air. As for us we have been loading our gear aboard too — instruments, gas masks, charts, goggles, films, nose swabs, and so on, checking and rechecking our lists a dozen times.

At noon, Commander Pew briefed the squadron once more, reminding each pilot of his identifying signals, and indicating minor changes in operational procedure. He was cool and matter-of-fact, and with a slow smile informed the crews that their pictures would be taken this afternoon, "so that they could remember what they looked like before the Geigers hit them."

This evening there was a marvelous sunset. Clouds had formed, as they often do here, directly over the islets of this atoll, stringing out in a similar broken chain overhead. In the unusual stillness of this evening, they persisted, between the flaming canopy of the sky and the copper cauldron of the lagoon, so solid, so stationary that one might wonder whether they were the mirror image of our islands, or we the image of the clouds.

Weather reports have been promising all day. B–29's head out on weather scouting missions several times daily, making a circuit far to the east and back. Tonight one came home with two of its four engines out and thick night close on its tail. No one has much thought of sleep.

ABLE DAY

Able Day — Monday, July 1, 1946

Our alarm clocks rang at 3:30. Last-minute reports showed that Able Day had arrived as scheduled. With the remainder of our gear we stumbled through the darkness to Squadron Headquarters, where the crews and pilots were gathering. My plane had been at her mooring all night, and so after digging up a few spare canisters for the gas masks I hiked across the cement apron to the wharf. In the faint light our giant birds were being trundled off to the launching ramp, their engines spitting bursts of fire and thunder in last-minute checks. I felt very small among such birds.

The B–29's were coming over, fire showing in their motors, and their wing lights blinking as they swept past. Down on the landing pier a motley invasion was taking place; hundreds of nonessential people from Kwajalein were coming ashore from their bobbing landing craft.

This was Able Day. What would happen when *Dave's Dream* hatched its famous egg? Would the prophecies they had read and heard be fulfilled — would pieces of our venerable Navy be spread all over the Pacific from the Philippines to Panama? Would a tidal wave sweep the islands clean and surge on to inundate Los Angeles? Would, indeed, the very water itself become involved in a chain reaction until the whole Pacific Ocean disappeared in a colossal eruption? Who was to say? Or who, at least, was to say No?

At any rate it appeared that the Kwajalein contingent had been celebrating the coming of the end of the world, for they reeled along the pier in noisy confusion and high spirits. Several fell or were pushed into the water, and one, we later heard, cracked his skull.

By 5:30 in the first light of dawn we were airborne, climbing slowly to 8000 feet and swinging away to the northwest. Dawn came and passed unnoticed. There was much to do, and the sweet singing of our twin motors, perfectly tuned for their day of work, seemed to warn that they would give me only a minimum of time to prepare. First there were the instruments on the navigation table. Turning them on, I tested each one with a small pocket radium source. Over the Geiger counters the clicks were coming in at their usual hundred or so counts per minute. The cosmic rays were manifesting no particular excitement over the approaching explosion.

Next there were the film badges, protective goggles, and gas masks to pass out to all hands. In spite of the distracting smell of steak coming from the galley, the crew welcomed their issue of strange gear. The little films, worn in the pocket, were sheer mystery to them; the goggles meant total darkness during the actual flash; but the gas masks they understood — despite the inconvenience of flying encumbered with such a device they were glad to have it.

By the time we had cleared away the steak and French fries, washed them down with a cup of scald and topped it all off with a cigarette, we were dropping down through the cottony cloud layers to Bikini. The live fleet was strung out in several columns under us, and some twenty miles away the target fleet was visible bunched up at one end of the lagoon. Our skipper, of course, had to pay his respects to the *Bountiful*. After that he flew on to Bikini in order to orient himself at our prescribed point of orbit. At 3000 feet we were running into a steady sea of fleecy clouds and there was some doubt in our minds whether the drop ship could make out the target.

However, we soon picked up the broadcast we had been waiting for. Calmly and slowly the bombardier aboard *Dave's Dream* was saying "This is Skylight One, Skylight One. Ten minutes before first simulated bomb release. Stand by. Mark: ten minutes before first simulated bomb release. First practice run."

It came through clear and sharp and instinctively we looked up even though we knew that Skylight One was too high to be visible. Radio silence had been ordered throughout the fleet so that all planes and ships could hear the big bomber.

"This is Skylight One, Skylight One," came the voice again. "Two minutes before simulated bomb release. Two minutes before simulated bomb release. Stand by. Mark: first practice run."

By this time, Commander Pew had checked in with the control ship and was lazily circling in his prescribed area. Since we were to work together, we fell in behind him about a half mile distant. The sight of another ship suddenly evoked a feeling of the loneliness of our mission. Everything to do with the task force had to be done by remote control. There was the target — twenty miles away to the southwest, barely visible in the hazy sunlight. There was part of the live fleet a good ten miles farther from the target than we. Overhead we knew the sky to be full of planes, some of them five or six miles aloft, and yet none were to be seen. The capricious radio was to be our only contact with the gigantic movement.

The voice from above called the one minute mark — then, "This is Skylight One, Skylight One. Coming up on simulated bomb release. Stand by. Mark: end of first practice run, first practice run." In our minds we could see the slim, silvery B–29 swinging slowly away to begin her next run. Would this be it?

As though in answer the calm voice said: "This is Skylight One, Skylight One. Predicted time of actual bomb release 30 minutes. Predicted time of actual release 30 minutes."

Then our control ship, Sadeyes, came in. "Skylight One, this is Sadeyes. Over."

The answer came at once: "Sadeyes, this is Skylight One. Over."

"Skylight One, this is Sadeyes. Interrogation: will you say how conditions were for bombing on your first practice run? Over."

"Sadeyes, this is Skylight One. Bombing conditions were okay [with a trace of satisfaction in the 'okay']. Over."

"Sadeyes to Skylight One. Roger — out!"

We made another sweep over the fleet. As in the rehearsal, the ships were strung out in Indian file and barely stirring up a green wake. You could see the people standing motionless at the rail, watching the faint smudge of Bikini Atoll on the horizon line. Even the smoke lazily tailing out from the stacks seemed intent upon the fateful island. For all the roar of our twin engines, everything seemed to be holding a breathless silence. Finally, after twenty minutes had passed and no sound had come from Skylight One, our radioman began to get the jitters. Suppose we shouldn't receive the word of the bomb drop, and were blinded by the flash. He began to spin his dials. What a relief when the words came through, calm as ever: "This is Skylight One, Skylight One. Five minutes before actual bomb release. Mark: five minutes before actual bomb release. Stand by."

Five minutes!

"Skylight One, Skylight One. Two minutes before actual bomb release. Mark: two minutes before actual bomb release. Adjust all goggles. Adjust all goggles. Stand by."

And then at last: "Coming up on actual bomb release. Stand by. . . . [an eternity] . . . Bomb away. Bomb away. Bomb away. Bomb away."

I began to count the seconds to myself. Skylight One would be up on one wing, going into a long curving dive so as to be miles away when its mysterious burden came to life. Meanwhile, our pilot had been fumbling with the controls, and I heard him mutter to his co-pilot: "Now wouldn't that frost you. I forgot to set this crate on automatic pilot. I must be getting to be an old man."

The seconds passed — 20 — our ship was now righted and flying away from the target under automatic pilot — 30 — nothing to be seen through the black goggles, and the pounding of one's heart made counting difficult — 35 — 40 — I suddenly realized I had been holding my breath since the time of the bomb release — 45 — 50 — 60 — nothing happened.

For us the Bomb went off unannounced. The ball of fire which had fused several acres of the New Mexico desert into glass and turned Hiroshima into a symbol of man's inhumanity burst over the target ships, seared the paint from their decks and melted down their masts, but at twenty miles gave us no sound or flash or shock wave.

Coming out from under we could discern no change in the world. Had it been a dud? Had we miscalculated the time now to be blinded by the flash? The radio was silent.

Then, suddenly we saw it — a huge column of clouds, dense, white, boiling up through the strato-cumulus, looking much like any other thunderhead but climbing as no storm cloud ever could. The evil mushrooming head soon began to blossom out. It climbed rapidly to 30,000 or 40,000 feet, growing a tawny-pink from oxides of nitrogen, and seemed to be reaching out in an expanding umbrella overhead. Although we were still 20 miles upwind, Lieutenant Lower cocked his eye up at it and called in a jittery voice: "Bradley, are you getting any Geigers here?"

"No, Skipper, nothing but the cosmics."

For minutes the cloud stood solid and impressive, like some gigantic monument, over Bikini. Then finally the shearing of the winds at different altitudes began to tear it up into a weird zigzag pattern. Winds high up were from the west and so the head tended to move out over us and menace the live fleet, while shreds of the torn column beneath could be seen moving slowly westward above the water.

Larson, in Commander Pew's plane, was apparently as worried about flying in under that plume as I was. We could hear him trying to make contact with the control ship, but the circuits by now were jammed.

Finally, we could not wait any longer; our duty was over the lagoon and we heard Lars's last exasperated message: "Sadeyes from Applejack One. Cancel all interrogation. Starting first sweep. Starting first sweep." Watching his plane streaking for Bikini Atoll beneath the low clouds I could imagine with what excitement they were adjusting their gas masks and checking their instruments. We turned and made a couple of sweeps over the live fleet just to reassure the senators and admirals, and then climbed to our specified altitude and headed for the tiny atoll.

For a long time we could see nothing. Someone ventured to suggest that all the ships had been sunk. But smoke at least was visible, moving slowly downwind. Then our pilot said, and his voice was something to hear: "Say, look, there's the *Sara* . . . still standing . . . beautiful, ain't she? Just like she was getting up steam to move out."

Soon after that we were able to make out the entire target area. Few ships, if any, had been sunk. Many of them were beginning to smoke and new fires seemed to be breaking out by the minute.

We were by now well under the tawny canopy. Nothing, however, had shown up on our instruments. The air was clear of fission products, which, carried aloft by the boiling updraft, would soon be joining those from the three other atomic bombs in the stratosphere. Then we heard Larson break through with the message:

"Leg three completed. Zero dose leg three."

That made us feel a lot better, and we decided to try to make our sweeps without gas masks. Things were hectic. We would fly a leg for a few minutes and then Lieutenant Lower would up-end his ship in a vertical bank, with the lagoon and its ships spinning like a pin wheel on the end of our wing, and we were off on the next leg. Up front the navigator, standing between the pilots, called our orientation points and checked the course for the skipper by the pattern of ships ahead. Back on the navigation table we had our instruments and our charts, where readings were made and plotted, and messages made out for the radioman to send on to Sadeyes.

Lars, transmitting on the same frequency, had found radiation, and we, as we approached the center of the target area, ran into it too. With a nervous sputter my Geiger counters came to life. At first it was patchy, seeming to be highest when we were passing over some ship. Toward dead center the ships were more closely bunched and there our counters really began to sing. Upon our first contact with radiation I had called over the interphone to the skipper to reassure him. Now with radiation a hundred times stronger I called him again: "Skipper, where are you now?"

"Coming in over the main target area."

"Well, we're really in it. Are we halfway through?"

"Just about. The *Nevada* is just ahead. Want to turn out?"

"No. It's not that bad yet. You could stick around here for several days if you had to."

"Thanks."

The *Nevada*, gaudy red forward and pretty well singed aft, turned out to be some distance from the most intense radiation, so we knew that *Dave's Dream* had not exactly scored a bull's-eye. We were flying low enough so that the ships passed rapidly beneath us and it was impossible to get more than a fleeting glimpse of them. Most of them seemed to be afire but not in critical condition. The apparent damage was surprisingly slight. The *Sara*, of course, had been wiped clear. Some of the cruisers and battleships had had their superstructures twisted and melted into a tangle of junk, and the light carrier *Independence* had been blown into a cocked hat. But otherwise the fleet looked as if it might survive.

Expecting much more dire and dramatic events our crew was disappointed. There was much pooh-poohing of the Bomb over the interphone, and at last the co-pilot growled: "Well, it looks to me like the atom bomb is just about like the Army Air Force — highly overrated."

Our first sweep went very well. There was nothing to be found in the air; the only radiation was coming up from the water and from the ships. Most of this was doubtless due to radiation induced in the central target ships themselves, for each one seemed to catch us in a beam, as though from a searchlight, as we passed overhead. However, up near the northwest corner we suddenly ran headlong into an unexpected jolt of radiation which made the counters sing. We were by that time miles away from the ships. Thinking that we might be running into an invisible streamer from the original cloud I called Lieutenant Lower:

"Monitor to Captain! Skipper I don't know what we just ran into but we're back in the hot stuff. See anything below?"

In a moment: "Nope — not a thing. No oil slick, no ships."

The co-pilot chimed in: "What about that smoke? We're just about downwind from those fires now. See it?"

That caused a spontaneous scramble for gas masks, and so for the next two hours, making surveys at lower altitudes, we huffed and puffed, sweated and cursed, and struggled with communications from the inside of the steamy masks. The radiation got progressively more intense as we came down, and, of course, the smoke got more generalized. However, the fires seemed to be pretty well self-limited, and we were thankful that no ships, loaded with ammo as they were, blew up beneath us.

By early afternoon our job was done, and we climbed out over the live fleet, which by now was approaching the atoll from the southeast. Warily and still in single file ships were lifting along, and the first of the small boats were already beginning to probe into the outer lagoon. These small boats were equipped with radio transmitters and batteries of Geiger counters. We did not envy the boarding parties their job; monitors and damage-control personnel would be sweating it out in heavy coveralls, boots, rubber gloves, and gas masks, boarding the big ships from those wet, greasy, jumping decks, and going below without lights or blowers, lugging their heavy equipment.

At last from Sadeyes came the welcome message: "Mission completed. Return to base." We had been in the air nearly twelve hours. Now that the tension was gone, everyone suddenly became tired and starved. No smoking and eating had been permitted during the surveys, lest anyone should thereby pick up dangerous material from the air. So a complete survey of the ship was in order. We discarded everything that had been open, all cigarette packs, bread, fruit, even the rest of that juicy steak. The boys took it pretty well, especially when I okayed a fresh gallon jar of olives and some canned beef. But not to be able to smoke — that was torture. Finally, Lieutenant Lower could stand it no longer:

"Bradley," he barked over the interphone, "how soon will I die if I smoke?"

"How old are you, Skipper?"

"Thirty."

"Oh, probably not for another thirty years."

"Well, hell, I'll die a lot sooner than that if I can't have a smoke."

After that we abandoned all conservative policy. The Captain ordered the ports to be opened to air out the ship, and we began to live like human beings again. Kwajalein looked as sunny and serene as ever as we circled for our approach.

By now, at sunset, the morning refugees are all back in Kwajalein, leaving Ebeye richer by the addition of a few drunks who sleep happily in the brig — but otherwise nothing seems to have been changed by the explosion of the fourth atomic bomb.

Tuesday, July 2

A solemn dawn, smelling of the approach of bad weather again. The tide was the lowest we have seen, leaving the entire shelf out to the barrier high and dry. The barrier reef itself was bare all up and down the length of the island. The long rollers were breaking up in foaming disarray.

Rumors from the big fleet indicate a general disappointment over the Bomb. The lagoon is still full of ships, and most of them have been safely boarded. Few have been sunk and not many are seriously damaged. Doubtless many people who have been fed on the fantasies regarding the Bomb will find Test Able something akin to K rations. Anything short of a second Krakatoa

would have been a letdown. Actually, of course, what
has happened is about what one would expect from an
air burst of the 1946 model atomic bomb. The damage
done to the ships should be largely to the superstructure,
not to the vital parts. The radioactivity now present on
board is probably mainly that induced in the metal by
the burst of neutrons at the moment of explosion.
Neutrons, like any other projectiles, have a limited
range, namely about 2000 yards in air, which is con-
siderably less than the area covered by the target
fleet.

It would appear that at least for the time being we have
escaped from the real threat of atomic weapons, namely
the lingering poison of radioactivity. The great bulk of
highly dangerous fission products was carried aloft into
the stratosphere where it can be diluted to the point of
insignificance in its slow fall-out. In this sense, therefore,
Test Able is very similar to the Hiroshima-Nagasaki
shots. The majority of damage will have been from
the blast wave, and probably only those experimental
animals exposed directly to the neutrons and gamma rays
at the moment of explosion will show the effects of
"atom bomb disease."

Our assignment in the air is over and soon we shall be
returning to Bikini. Last night one of the boys went out
in a B–29 to help locate the cloud. They had no trouble
finding it, a couple of hundred miles northwest of the
atoll, its radioactive mists still full of thrills for the

Geiger counters. Fortunately, the cloud passed far enough to the north so as not to threaten Eniwetok. It will be followed a few days longer by surface craft, and, of course, all but Crossroads shipping has been cleaned out of this area.

Upon her return to Kwajalein last night it was found that the big plane had been souvenir hunting. Her four motors were coated with radioactive material; so she is grounded and in quarantine. The rest of the handsome fleet of 29's is already preparing for the flight home. We shall miss their silvery sweeping flight, and the clear, matter-of-fact voice of the bombardier from Skylight One.

Wednesday, July 3

Back to Bikini and the *Haven*. Able plus two — already the lagoon is packed with shipping, as though where the Bomb had struck down one ship two had risen in its place. The shore, the water, and most of the ships are now considered to be radiologically safe. Having thus got off so lightly on Test Able, everyone seems to be in a festive mood. The beaches and bars were packed all afternoon; the poker games, enshrouded in a penumbra of smoke and profanity, have settled down for the night, and even the worst of pictures in Hollywood's dismal repertoire receives an unstinted acclaim. The lights about our *Haven* tonight give more the impression of a city than of a harbor.

Thursday, July 4

(The nation's birthday — celebrated by a full course turkey dinner.)

I had a lucky assignment today, that of accompanying a group of Navy photographers while they took pictures of the entire target fleet. We went aboard no ships but had a chance to examine at close hand the superficial damage evident on deck. No one seems to know how many ships were actually sunk — only a few at the most. However, some of the ships have been towed away and beached because they appeared to be in danger of foundering. Three of these we saw — the submarine *Skate*, the destroyer *Hughes*, and a cement seagoing dry dock — beached side by side near Enyu Island to await further study.

One sees plenty of evidence of the fury of that blast wave. The light carrier *Independence* is an impressive edifice of junk: its flight deck exploded, its hangar deck caved in, and all the complicated gadgetry of gun mounts, gangways, and electronic gear blown away or left dangling oversides in fantastic disarray. The ancient battleship *Arkansas*, lacking most of its superstructure aft of the bridge, looks well on the way to being modernized. It wouldn't take more than an ordinary bomb to turn her into a carrier. Similarly, the cruisers *Pensacola* and *Salt Lake City* have their superstructures torn loose and wrenched half oversides. The decks of these ships are a shambles. Overturned airplanes, wrecked lifeboats, and all sorts of debris are strewn around.

The sight of these ships reminded me of some buildings standing near the site of the first atomic bomb test in New Mexico. "Near" is used in the Pickwickian sense of being near enough — namely about four miles from the blast center. One building had been blown two feet across its cement foundation. Another, a barnlike structure, had taken the blast wave full on its sloping roof. It was pretty well mauled. Similarly here, the damage seems to be so haphazard and occasionally so violent as to suggest the action of some primordial force beyond one's comprehension.

And so, of course, it must be. The energy released in the explosion of an atomic bomb is that mysterious energy which holds nuclei of atoms together. The unstable uranium or plutonium nucleus requires a vast amount of energy to hold it together, whereas the binding energy required to hold together a smaller, more stable atom like barium is proportionately much less. It is this excess of nuclear energy which is given off (since it is no longer needed) when fission takes place and the heavy, unstable atom breaks down into several smaller, stable units.

The nature of this enormous force is, so far as I know, not understood. But we are beginning to learn about its magnitude here on earth. The sun has known about it for a long time; according to modern physicists the energy involved and evolved in the "burning" of the sun comes from the transformation of hydrogen atoms into helium atoms. At temperatures and pressures available on earth both of these atoms appear to be stable. But, according to hypothesis, at temperatures and pressures within the sun, hydrogen is unstable, its nucleus tending to combine and be transformed into the more stable helium nucleus. With this transformation comes the release of vast amounts of nuclear energy, given off as radiant energy, among which is the wave length of visible light.

That one should look to the sun for the nearest analogy of an explosion over Bikini Atoll should not surprise anyone. The solar system is after all but a tiny nebula in the glittering emptiness of the black heavens. The atom and the universe — these are the playthings of modern physicists.

Saturday, July 6

One of the most damaged of all ships is the submarine *Skate*. The sub had been dealt a double blow — first, by the Bomb, and second, by the newspapermen. In a bomb test disappointingly lacking in the spectacular, the press had rejoiced to find in the *Skate* a ship that had been truly blown "all to hell." And judging from its superstructure they were right. The gun emplacements were sheared clean off, the deck ripped up and heaved oversides. The twin periscopes were bent to an angle of 40 degrees, and amid a jungle of debris the forward gun mount had been turned around 180 degrees. The press had, therefore, long since buried the *Skate* under a deluge of words, if not of blue water.

However, to a man the crew felt differently. Translated from Navy lingo, they were saying: "What does the press know about pigboats? . . . roaring up in a skimmer with some three striper to take a few pictures topsides. . . . Who said she was sinking? . . . A week now and she hasn't taken in enough water to boil an egg in. . . . Wrecked? She'll sail off'n this reef under her own power."

The *Skate* was lying half a mile from shore, her bow resting on the bottom in about two and a half fathoms of water, and her stern free, gently lifting on the incoming swells. A big repair tug steamed up alongside, letting over some oxyacetylene cutting equipment with which the loose plates and twisted members of the superstructure and forward deck could be cut away. Finally the hatches were opened. Several of us, equipped with oxygen rebreathing apparatus, descended into the darkness and stale air of the after companionway. One by one the bulkheads were opened; each time the compartment ahead was tested for chlorine, carbon dioxide, freon, and for radioactivity, and finally declared safe. This continued until the entire ship was found to be safe. Then the blowers were started, and the engineers could go below.

The *Skate* must have been very close to the explosion. Nevertheless, her double-shelled, cigar-shaped hull was still tight, and the engines and batteries intact. The blast must have rolled her flat. Most of the dishes in the galley were smashed, and the officers' quarters were littered with broken phonograph records, pictures, books, and papers.

Once the gangways and compartments were open the crew really went to work. Someone found an American Flag and ran it up on one of the sprung periscope tubes, then a commissioning flag was set from the other.

The men had magnificent beards trimmed around the neck in the style of Yankee sea captains. Stripped to the waist, and smoking cigars or munching on apples, they beavered away. One could not distinguish the officers from the men — in dress, beard, activity, or language — except by the use of the word "Mister." It was hard work, like resuscitating a half-drowned man, but with every hour's accomplishment they gained in confidence that their ship would come back to life. The chilly showers, alternating with a broiling sun, went entirely unnoticed, and as the work progressed spirits rose, more apples and cigars appeared, and a rich and joyous profanity invested every communication.

At last the *Skate* was ready. Bow tanks were blown out and her slim nose began to swing and grate on the coral. Then the engines began to vibrate beneath us, and the twin propellers began their irresistible slow rotation.

As slick as on her first launching the *Skate* came off the reef, and an hour later was steaming triumphantly through the fleet. She could not be steered from the conning tower; instead the skipper balanced himself there and shouted his commands down through the hatch to the control room below.

Dusk was coming on by the time he had cruised through the fleet and found his sub tender. Obviously enjoying all the formalities, he called his signal man to flash them a message requesting permission to anchor. This was done with a flashlight, and at once the mother ship replied. Then the chains came rattling from their wells, the anchor splashed, and we were berthed. Colors were called, all hands standing to attention while the flag was hauled down from the wrecked periscope. Riding lights were set and the mate posted his watches, and thus the now famous *Skate* was officially "secured" for the night.

Not long after that my Higgins boat arrived to take me back to the *Haven*. The Captain waved his thanks and, still smiling, went below. And it was more than the smell of grilling steak, rising from the hatches, which made him smile.

Sunday, July 7

Test Able is almost a thing of the past. The evil cloud born a week ago tomorrow has dissipated itself in the northwest and no longer needs to be followed; the water of Bikini lagoon is considered entirely safe, and most of the ships have been thoroughly inspected both for structural damage and for radioactivity. They are already being towed into position for the next round. Scientists of many specialties have been all over the area making observations, picking up samples, and detaching souvenirs.

One of the fellows in the bunkroom had collected a chunk of metal from the ship considered to have been nearest to the blast. He had it stowed away in his locker beside the bed. Then one day somebody was checking a Geiger counter in the vicinity and began to pick up a strong emission. At once he tracked down and located the loot and showed its anxious owner that he'd been sleeping in a shower of gamma rays. The queerest stuff turns up radioactive: a ship's bell of brass; some chemicals from a first-aid locker on deck; and a bar of soap that had been caught in a stream of neutrons. You never can tell what insignificant thing will bear the invisible brand of the Bomb. Souvenirs of all kinds have been forbidden throughout the task force, but that's too much to expect of human nature.

Today I had a chance to observe some of the footprints of the mighty cloud as it passed over the western end of Bikini Atoll. All of the tiny islets and sandspits on the far end of Bikini are uninhabited; nevertheless, they have to be officially cleared. Lieutenant Allan Bott, a naval fighter pilot and recent addition to the Radiological Safety Section, and I were glad to get the assignment.

Early in the morning, a PGM (a Patrol Gun Boat) hove to alongside and picked us up. After an hour's run to the westward end of the atoll we raised our first island — called Cherry, because its native name is unpronounceable. Merely a low rocky shelf, it is separated from its neighbor by a deck of shallows, and is unapproachable from all directions save by a narrow passage. This passage lies between the shoals on the lagoon side, and surging white water of the barrier reef along the ocean side. At that one point the eddying waters have built out a sandspit, and surrounded it with clear green water.

The skipper had a dinghy put over the side to which an outboard motor was rigged. Then five of us — two sailors, an oceanographic man, and Bott and I — dropped in and were cast off. To say that we were left to the mercy of the elements would be to pass the buck. One of the sailors had never rowed a skiff in his life. He decided that the best way to take the big waves was to swing broadside to them, which nearly cost us our instruments with the first comber. Then the outboard, true to the best traditions, couldn't be made to run. While the man in the stern whipped the motor with a frenzy of curses, the oarsman in the bow decided to pull directly for the island. But by this time the wind had set us well into the channel between the islands and such a course would have taken us for a joy ride on the surf that was foaming over the curving barrier reef. Things can really get out of hand in a tiny overloaded skiff on a choppy sea. Bott and I at last decided to waive Navy courtesies, took over the oars and headed unheroically for the open sea. Eniwetok 175 miles away looked better than that barrier reef. Finally the motor dried out and was coaxed into sputtering activity. A little timorously we splashed back through the pass and gained the sandy beach.

Brilliant coral sand, hot, glaring, radiant — and back of it a fine grove of trees. The oceanographer had installed certain instruments prior to Test Able by which he hoped to tell whether or not the atoll had changed in any way by the violence of the blast. While he went off to make his readings, Bott and I struck off inland. It was a beautiful little island, less than half a mile across, covered entirely with a breezy open pandanus glade, and having a single grove of coconut palms at the far point.

At Bikini, Ebeye, and Kwaj, one almost never sees birds. But Cherry proved to be a rookery; birds rose in screaming protest all about us and the trees were burdened with their nests. Terns they were — black noddy terns and dainty little fairy terns, pure white and almost translucent against the sky. They were clearly the sole proprietors of the little island, else they would not have dared to be so careless about their nests. These nests were a jumble of sticks, hopelessly untidy, having almost no concavity, and built right over the top of previous nests. The dry, broken shells of a past generation lie in the same shallow depression with the eggs of the next. Such are the nests of the noddy terns. The fairy tern is even less preoccupied with household duties. She lays her single egg in a convenient fork of a limb and then goes about her social engagements, leaving to the constant sun the duties of incubation.

It was clear that the great cloud had passed this way. Small amounts of radioactive materials had come down in its rainy tresses. Even below the high water mark, on the south shore, whose rocky ledges are constantly being sluiced by the foaming breakers, even here we found radioactive material, invisibly and almost permanently adsorbed to the surface of the rocks. It isn't enough to be serious, but illustrates the difficulty of trying to clean any rough surface of fission products. Even the great Pacific itself cannot wash out a roentgen of it.

The lagoon side of little Cherry has more to tell of the Bikini tests than incidental radioactivity. There the full story of man's coming is spread out on the beach: boxes, mattresses, life belts, tires, boots, bottles, broken-up landing craft, rusting machinery and oil drums, all the crud and corruption of civilization spread out on the sands, and smeared over with inches of tar and oil.

We found the same conditions on Oruk and the other islands we visited. In the lavish expense account for Operation Crossroads, the spoilage of these jeweled islets will not even be mentioned, but no one who visited them could ever forget it.

Wednesday, July 10

For the past several days diving operations have been going on in the target area, where several ships have been sunk, and with them a number of scientific instruments to register blast pressures, and neutron intensities. Today it was my luck to monitor aboard one of the tugs when they hit a jack pot down below. The ship was a solid grimy seagoing bucket made for submarine rescue work, skippered by a tall, quiet, competent fellow, and manned by a hearty crew of profane giants. Previous diving attempts had located the hull of the sunken ship, above which the tug was now securely moored fore and aft. Those who had seen the hulk in the milky twilight of the lagoon floor described her as being broken in three pieces and almost unrecognizable as a ship. The divers at least are satisfied that the Bomb is not an overrated weapon.

The morning proved windy and too rough for diving operations, but by noon the wind had let go, and the sea was glassy hot. Four divers began getting into their complicated suits. They were big burly extroverts, with rough solid names — Marsh, Eichorn, Red Baith, and Goring (known as Herman, of course). There was certainly no fear in them; claustrophobia was too fancy a neurosis for them to bother with.

Baith and Herman were soon ready. In their elaborate costumes, weighing well over two hundred pounds, they looked like medieval sea monsters floundering about on land. Jockeyed into position on a steel platform, they were then hoisted over the side. After testing their suits in the water they were quickly lowered to the bottom of the lagoon, some 185 feet down, a great green plume of bubbles swirling up from their escape valves. We couldn't get Herman on the phone, but Baith called up saying that they had landed near the bow of the sunken ship, that Herman was starting off in search of the missing instruments, while he, Baith, would stand by to keep his lines clear.

Herman was carrying a special watertight Geiger tube fashioned in a long brass probe and transmitting to a counter on deck. Almost at once I began to get indications of radioactivity. At one point the indicator needle went clear off scale. We called down to Baith to find out what Goring was doing.

"I think he's resting," came the reply. "At least he's sitting down."

"Well, what is he sitting on?"

"Looks like a stanchion, maybe."

"Then tell him to stand clear. The Geiger man says it's hot." I should like to have seen Goring make his leap from the hot seat; we could hear Baith laughing at it. Then the skipper lowered a hook to the bottom and took the brass stanchion aboard as a specimen.

After a long interval Baith excitedly called and said that Herman had found the instruments all strung together on a cable. They, too, were soon hoisted overside and proved to be exactly what the Navy was looking for. They looked harmless enough, but a survey soon indicated that no one could be allowed on the fantail of the tug until the loot was taken over by the proper authorities.

Life aboard a tug is dirty, grimy, intimate, and comfortable. Chow is excellent. We had *filet mignon* with mushrooms for lunch. There is no show of formality. The skipper is out there heaving on the lines and doing the same work as the seamen. The only thing that distinguishes the old man from his crew is the age in his face and the mildness of his language. These ships seem to have an ample supply of mascots. In addition to a dog and cat this one had a pet monkey who endeared himself to the crew by biting all strangers, regardless of race, religion, or rank.

Long after dark Baith and Goring were still sitting on the platform underwater, being decompressed, and making five dollars an hour plus their base pay. We knew they were all right from the whirling nebulae of bubbles, and from the occasional calls they made to ask what dinner was to be, or about the latest baseball scores.

By the time our LCP(L) came to take us back to the *Haven* a three-quarter moon was rising high over the target fleet. It was a beautiful sight, with luminous clouds drifting by overhead and the fleet, black and impressive, riding at anchor, blinking their messages back and forth. Some battlewagon, far on the other side of the anchorage, was signaling with the intense blue light of the new carbon arc lamps. The weird light came streaming through the massive silhouette of the *Nagato*'s fire-control tower like the groping fingers of some unearthly will. And so this Bikini fleet has often seemed to be at night.

Friday, July 12

Ebeye again. Assignments for the next test were given out last night, and the seaplane base is our home once more. Our group has changed a little. Charlie, Tom, Larson, and I remain of the previous group. Bott has a Carrier assignment, and in place of him we have a trio of Navy buzz-boys.

We are glad to be back, glad for the squadron's warm welcome, and for the somnolent days of sunny Ebeye. Ebeye is only 175 miles from Bikini, yet it seems more remote from the cares and complexities of the world than the Land of the Lotus Eaters. Days and nights have no wishes to fulfill; life could hardly be more amnesic than in our simple Quonset hut, whose window is the near full moon and whose doorstep is the barrier reef.

Tuesday, July 16

Low tide and a full moon tonight. "Mac, the Marine" — a former Marine gone native and working here in a sort of American trading post — dropped in to see if anyone wanted to go lobster fishing. Lobsters out here are enormous, and beautifully patterned with blue-green, purple, and ivory colors. They are said to live in the caverns of the outer reef and at night to come up to feed on the tidewater shelf inside the barrier. Standard equipment for lobster fishing appears to be a Coleman lamp, shorts, gloves, GI boots, a club or spear, a bottle of "Jugeroo," and a willingness to part with one's complexion in flying tackles in shallow water. The most important item is, of course, the Jugeroo, a native brand of cough medicine made of fermented coconut juice. A few sublethal swigs of Jugeroo will turn the most diffident zoologist into an all-American tackle.

So we went. The shelf was practically bare and we could hike out nearly to the next island. We sloshed along knee-deep in water, just inside the spume where visibility is poor. After a couple of rain squalls had worked us over, the lamp went out. It was no match for the moon anyway, and so we abandoned it for the native style of fishing.

Mac turned out to be an interesting if somewhat optimistic Waltonian. He had been through the campaigns of Saipan, Iwo, and Okinawa, but was completely unemotional about them. Having given up the idea early of ever getting through the war alive, he had gone ahead and done his job in a detached sort of way. His recollections are a sort of scrapbook where banzai charges, Ernie Pyle, night patrols, geisha girls, beachheads, flame throwers, and Okinawan mistresses are all cluttered together, unassorted and unlabeled. He spoke of them all in the same impersonal way in which they had happened at the time.

I cannot say whether our technique for lobster hunting was the best. At any rate we didn't flush any, and only by heroic efforts managed to chase one terrified fish up onto the beach. Perhaps, as Mac suggested, the moon was too bright. I'm sure it was never more beautiful. We enjoyed it, slogging along knee-deep in quicksilver, with the mysterious Pacific muttering away among the crevasses and caverns of the reef, and the waves sweeping in over the shallows, like bolts of lace unrolling on the beach.

Wednesday, July 17

One of our compatriots here on Ebeye is Alexander Forbes, former Captain in the Navy, who will be flying with us to study and photograph the tidal wave expected in the next test. Forbes, one of the foremost physiologists of his time, was called early into research on the physiology of high altitude flying. He was soon transferred, by urgent request, to consult on the oceanographic details of building a large airfield in Labrador. Later he had duty in the Aleutians in the problem of navigation and airstrip engineering. Eventually he became a specialist in aerial photography and in this capacity he is here, in charge of a whole field of research in the wave phenomena of atomic explosions.

There is a nice story about Dr. Forbes which has made the rounds of Task Force One. It seems that prior to the Able Day test he wished to make a personal inspection of all stationary camera equipment on Bikini Atoll. These cameras were huge devices installed at the tops of steel towers located on several of the islets of the atoll. Needing assistance, he took with him a big, burly, somewhat overfed Marine photographer. The Marine was glad to have such an assignment: "Me go along with that white-haired gent? Sure. He'll probably spend most of the day under a palm tree somewhere!"

This illusion was soon shattered. Dr. Forbes is slender and white-haired, and quite hard of hearing, but these are the only concessions he has made to his age. No sooner had his gig touched the wharf at Bikini than he leaped ashore, and headed straight cross-country, taking the dense underbrush at a lope. Up the first tower he scrambled as though taking in the topsails for a squall. By the time the puffing Marine had struggled to the top, Dr. Forbes had finished inspecting the cameras and their radio-control mechanisms, and was on his way down. And so it went for the rest of the Bikini towers.

This done, he turned his gig for Amen Island, where more towers were located, and finally to Enyu. That evening a prostrate Marine was carried back to his ship. He was drenched with sweat, and swore that he'd lost twenty pounds. "Tarawa was never like this," he gurgled.

Friday, July 19

"William Day" — dress rehearsal for the underwater test — certainly began for us completely underwater. Never has there been such a rain. It started at 1:00 A.M. with the tin roof of our Quonset sounding as though a million demented drummers were gathered on it for a jam session. Floods poured through the windows in horizontal gusts. Fitful flashes of lightning, rare down here, and the booming of thunder, finished off all sleep. We swam in our beds, cursed, and wondered whether our planes could ever survive such a beating.

Spot time on the ramp was 4:15. Arising half an hour early, we staggered out, floundering now and then in the morass of the flooded road, and were amazed to find lights burning, and motors warming up. Crews were busy everywhere, shouting to each other in the darkness, and one by one the giant birds were being trundled down the flooded apron to the launching ramp, where, with a final crescendo, the engines were checked. Then down the ramp they went, till borne on the buoyant black water, where the wheels were released and the birds became creatures of flight once more.

By 6:00 the squadron was airborne, strung out through the squalls on the way to Bikini. Charlie Wells is flying with me for this test, and Lars in Commander Pew's ship will have Tom Madden. This will make it possible to get much better readings of radioactivity than were possible on Test Able. Charlie wasn't very familiar with the interphone system and was trying the gadget out on Lieutenant Lower. An energetic and high-geared little fellow, Charlie talked so fast that no one could understand him:

"Can you hear me? Can you hear me?" he chirped in his high nervous voice. Getting no answer, he remembered his communications jargon: "Monitor to Pilot. Monitor to Pilot. How do you read me? How do you read me?"

"Monitor, I hear you fine," returned the pilot, "but what's on your mind?"

"Monitor to Pilot," shouted Charlie with a gleam of triumph, "I know it must be hard for you to understand, hard to understand, I only wanted to make sure you could hear me."

Of course by this time everyone on the ship was listening to the crazy conversation the skipper was having with the Geiger man. Charlie was a clay pigeon waiting to be shot down, and these pilots never miss any chance for gunnery practice.

"Sure I get you, Doc," drawled our pilot in high glee. "You sound just like a little chicken inside an egg."

The storm which had hit us at midnight today was working Bikini over. It was an impossible day for an air rehearsal, and after circling around for a couple of hours, somewhat on edge because our starboard engine was sputtering, we received orders to return to base.

Sunday, July 21

Fortunately on Sunday the Shore Patrol believes in resting, and then one may, with luck, explore the reef from scientific or aesthetic curiosity with relative safety. By good fortune I ran into a Marine photographer who, equipped with steel spear, spear gun, and goggles, was just starting out for some reef fishing. The tide was dead low and the whole reef stretched in a jagged barricade along the outside of the islands. Between it and the actual land is a tidewater shelf which is perhaps a half mile in width; here the water is warm and stagnant, and the dead coral scummed over with slime. The barrier itself is several feet higher, made up of living coral and calciferous algae and kept alive by the constant wash of the surf.

From the shore the barrier reef looked as solid and secure as a line of tank traps. As we neared it we kept seeing flashes of brilliant blue-green in the water ahead, and these we discovered, as the water began to shoal again, were schools of parrot fish. Hoping to drive them up on the barrier reef and capture some of the gaudy creatures we began to run. But just as it seemed certain that we should beach the whole school in one mad rush, they all miraculously vanished. Only then did we realize what we were standing on — the thin, shell-like roof which covered the honeycombed outer reef! Far from a substantial footing, the coral was cut up into innumerable passages, gullies, and canyons down which the parrot fish had made their getaway. The sea was all about us, and under us, heaving and sighing and muttering to itself. Through the crevasses and wells it would come surging up and sucking back, ebbing and flowing, until one could believe that the land itself was alternately rising and sinking to a deep troubled rhythm.

Beyond the outcroppings which make up the actual barrier reef, the coral begins to sink away rapidly into the ultramarine of the deep Pacific. Shoal water extends out for only a hundred feet or so, and in this area the long Pacific swells peak themselves up and come lunging in in an avalanche of foam. When the surf is running high, swimming would be unthinkable, but fortunately today the sea was calm, and by waiting for a quiet spell between the bigger waves one could easily swim out beyond the breakers along any one of the large channels which cut the outer reef into a series of jagged ribs.

That barricade of coral and white water is the threshold to a new world, one totally unsuspected and unimaginable from above. Once beneath the surface you enter a land enchanted. Mountains and weird coral castles stand all around you, fading away in the opalescent distance. Caverns and canyons lead away into the terrifying chasm of deep water, and over their sandy bottoms the sunlight passes like flowing tile. Here in the shallows, beneath the sky that passes in clouds of bubbles, are myriads of exotic fish, passing along the corridors and caverns in schools that ebb and flow like the currents. Blunt-nosed parrot fish hover in the near distance, their scales like iridescent blue mail. Surgeon fish, wearing respectable gray and black, with a dash of orange back of the gills, pass in idle curiosity; coppery squirrel fish, flirtatious damsel fish, and the beautiful shy Moorish idols — these and many other species flit around you among the coral heads.

At a distance you may catch sight of a school of jacks, so nearly transparent that you may wonder if they are hallucinations until they turn and the sun glints from their sides as though from polished steel. These fish show no fear unless you menace them; to them you are only a new fish, somewhat awkward and funny looking, to be sure, but still an acceptable citizen of the reef.

We saw none of the dangerous Moray eels, and only a few small sand shark, curious but cowardly creatures, which came sniffing around at a safe distance to see what was going on. My companion, the Marine, proved to be a skilled archer with his catapult and steel spears. I could hear his arrows clinking on the rocks, but in the end he had a respectable catch of fish hanging from his belt. The edible ones we later cooked on the beach, Marshallese style — that is, over hot stones. What they lacked of the Duncan Hines touch was easily made up for with a bottle of the local tongue-blight, Jugeroo. And so has passed another day, as remote from the impending atomic bomb as could be imagined.

Wednesday, July 24

Baker Day minus one has been very much like Able Day minus one. Commander Pew called the squadron together for a final briefing and a parting word of confidence. We Geiger men tried to describe in a rough way what was expected to happen in a shallow-water blast. But honestly, who knows? Who can predict? We will have to take our chances with the unexpected.

Tom and Lars, Charlie and I, have checked and rechecked our instruments, our gas masks, and all the rest of the paraphernalia and nothing seems to have been overlooked. Nevertheless one cannot suppress a feeling of excitement mixed with a dash of anxiety when one considers the possibilities of tomorrow's test. The four previous atomic bombs have been exploded in air, so that the majority of the radioactive material produced as fission products has been swept up into the remote and harmless stratosphere.

But this will be entirely different. The bomb is suspended beneath an LCI, and will be detonated electrically. The actual depth beneath the surface is not known to us. It cannot be more than the 180-foot depth of the lagoon, and will probably be much less. Scientists who are familiar with the magnitude of atomic forces predict that a chimney of water half a mile in diameter will be thrown up many thousands of feet. Tons and tons of water will be vaporized to steam by the intense heat, and will then condense into a cloud around the top of the chimney. Whereas the cloud in the Able test climbed rapidly to 30,000 feet, the cloud this time is not expected to go half so high. Instead, it will at once begin to rain down upon the target area, and the rain will certainly be deadly from the entrapped fission products.

As the giant pillar of salt water begins to fall, and the great hole in the lagoon fills in, a wave will form around the base; rolling out like an enormous tidal wave, it will engulf the target fleet and then sweep on to the islands. Predictions vary as to the magnitude of this wave. Some say that all the ships will be turned over and sunk, and the entire atoll swept clear of vegetation. More conservative opinion among oceanographers doubts that the wave, by the time it has traveled the seven miles to Bikini Island, will have force enough to carry it across the island.

Most thinking leads to fanciful predictions of physical violence. But of much greater concern to us of the Radiological Safety Section is that rain of radioactive fission particles. The Colonel in his picturesque offhand way states that the radioactivity will be "the equivalent of tons of radium." When one considers that one millionth of a gram of radium contained within the body may be fatal one is inclined to turn from calculus to Christianity for comfort.

Fortunately this intense radioactivity will not remain at such an astronomical level. The half life of many of the fission components is but a few minutes or a few days. Nevertheless, we are inclined to take our cue from Dr. Hirschfelder, our task force oracle, who says that the ships will not be safe to go aboard for months.

Under the circumstances, should we pray for a dud? No such luck. A complete dud is unlikely in the nature of the bomb, and a partial explosion would be more dangerous than a total explosion. A partial explosion would spread plutonium all over the ships and the lagoon. Plutonium is a far more deadly and insidious hazard than fission products for two reasons: first, it is very hard to detect with field instruments. Since it is an alpha-particle emitter, our Geiger-Müller counters and ionization chambers will not detect its presence. A special and extremely delicate "alpha counter" is necessary for such work, and here at Bikini, under field conditions, no such alpha counter would survive a single day's work.

The second reason why plutonium contamination is so much to be feared is that its lethal action is roughly the same as that of radium. It lodges in the bones, destroys the blood-producing marrow, and may kill its host by wrecking his red and white blood cells; or, if the host survives that early period, he may die years later from bone tumors. In some respect plutonium appears to be more dangerous than an equivalent amount of radium, because, unlike the latter, once lodged in the bones, plutonium cannot be removed by processes known to medical science to date.

Well, this is all useless speculation anyway. There is no way to prevent tomorrow from coming, any more than one can detain time and the sunset, which now lights our island, our planes, and our crowded lagoon with its rosy radiance. As though to toast this special evening, the sunset has thrown a perfect rainbow over all the eastern panorama, its splendor seeming to hint that though your feet may be tangled in night, there is no limit to the earth's beauty if you will but raise your eyes.

Yes, tomorrow comes, heralded by a new type of sunrise gun. In the words of the old spiritual: "There's no hidin' place" down here.

July 1, 1946. Bikini Atoll. Test Able, a low-level airburst over eastern end of the atoll. The shockwave in water and the hemisphere of fog following the shockwave in the air are clearly shown. Enyu island nearby, Bikini island in the distance.

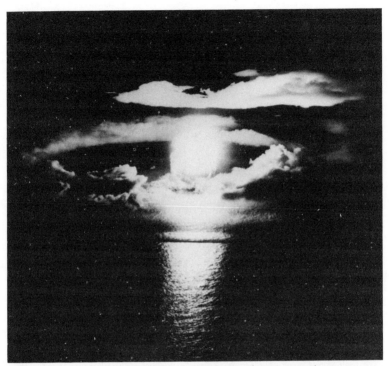

The fireball arising. A light as bright as the sun at the surface of the sun. So beautiful, so deadly.

Diver with a geiger probe searching for instruments torn from the decks of the target ships.

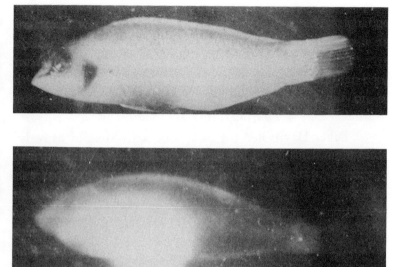

Bikini wrasse, a bottom feeder. The lower picture was made by splitting the fish, drying one half and placing it upon photographic film. Beta and gamma radiation, concentrated in the fish's gills, stomach, intestine, liver, and reproductive organs, create a sunburst on the film.

BAKER DAY

Baker Day called for us at 3:00 A.M. Most of us had only cat-napped anyway. Down at the pilots' ready room the officers were gathering. A percolator was producing some black and bitter brew, which we accepted as coffee. Outside, the darkness was filled with the roar of revving engines; showers of sparks were blowing down across the apron. When spot time arrived, Charlie and I made our way down across the deck searching for our plane. In the faint light of the machine shops the best way to identify a ship is by the mascot painted upon the high gray nose. Most of them are girls in varying degrees of exposure — Varga Girls, Caniff queens, and so on. Our ship, however, has only a number. It is known as the *Flying Dutchman*, because Lieutenant Lower and six of his nine men are from Pennsylvania.

The flight to Bikini seemed to pass more quickly than usual. There was lots to do in the way of giving out film badges and gas masks, in checking our six instruments. Dawn, as beautiful and brief as ever, came and went almost unnoticed.

Soon we found the live fleet under us, coasting along as before in Indian file, barely leaving a green wake. The weather was ideal, and planes were checking in from all parts of the sky. "Wet Paint" at the task force control station informed us that we were to use a wind axis of 140 degrees true in our survey. Larson in the other ship returned them a brief "Roger," and relayed the instructions to us. Now and then, from the control center of the fleet came the solemn Harvard accent of the man who would detonate the bomb.

"One owah befoah How Owah. One owah befoah How Owah."

That hour passed rapidly. Our skipper couldn't resist the temptation to drag all the ships at masthead height "to give all those admirals a feelin' of security." So down he went, pausing as always to circle the white-sided *Bountiful*, then off to play leapfrog with the file of ships. "Golly, what a gunnery run," Lieutenant Lower shouted to the co-pilot. "Ka-ka-ka-ka" he roared. "Ka-ka-ka-ka — Fire one — BOOM. Ka-ka-ka-ka — Fire two — BOOM. Nice work, torpedoman, you just sank Tojo's private yacht." And the crew all smiled to each other, thinking: "Well, boys, the old man's busted loose again."

Finally the Harvard accent came back on the air again:

"Ten minutes befoah How Owah. Ten minutes befoah How Owah."

Commander Pew was circling at the appointed station, about 15 miles northeast of the target, and we dropped in behind him.

"Five minutes befoah How Owah." No goggles were necessary for the underwater test, since the ultraviolet rays would be filtered out in the water. The Marine photographer in the waist opened up his hatches, and set up his bulky camera gear. At the one minute mark, our two planes straightened into a tangential course. The crew crowded to the ports, fixing their eyes upon the faint outlines of the Bikini ships sketched on the horizon.

And so "How Owah" arrived, according to plan and to the split second. I suppose from this task force will come 42,000 different descriptions. Yet the sum total of them all couldn't give the true impression of the suddenness and the magnitude of that explosion. The calm and implacable voice was saying:

"Ten seconds . . . five seconds . . . four seconds . . . three . . . two . . . one."

What his last word was I have no idea, nor can I tell what the color of that flash was. To me it was red; Lars swears that it was white. I have seen two hundred pounds of T.N.T. go off at night from a distance of half a mile, but this shot in broad day, at fifteen miles, seemed to spring from all parts of the target fleet at once. A gigantic flash — then it was gone. And where it had been now stood a white chimney of water reaching up and up. Then a huge hemispheric mushroom of vapor appeared like a parachute suddenly opening. It rapidly filled out in all directions until it struck the level of the first layer of clouds, about 1800 feet. Here, as though striking a layer of plate glass, this shock wave (or more strictly speaking, this cloud of vapors which formed in the vacuum phase behind the shock wave) spread out by leaps and bounds beneath the clouds. I remember being alarmed lest our plane be overtaken and smashed by it.

By this time the great geyser had climbed to several thousand feet. It stood there as if solidifying for many seconds, its head enshrouded in a tumult of steam. Then slowly the pillar began to fall and break up. At its base a tidal wave of spray and steam arose, to smother the fleet and move on toward the islands.

All this took only a few seconds, but the phenomenon was so astounding as to seem to last much longer. With the final disappearance of the column of water, the lagoon became obscured in a sallow rain cloud. For nearly twenty minutes the cloud hung like an evil curse over the ships. Eventually, however, the steady trades prevailed and the synthetic storm moved away to the northwest. One by one, the ships emerged, and when at last the long gray silhouette of the *Saratoga* was seen breaking out of the mist we all began to feel more at home. The *Nevada*, the black *Nagato*, the *New York*, and many others were soon identifiable, but the *Arkansas*, that bluff old battlewagon, had disappeared for good.

By thirty minutes after the shot most of the area was

clear again and we could see the fleet still riding at anchor, miraculously unchanged. An oily slick was spreading out from the center and mixed with it was a ghoulish green stain. This dismal color put everyone on edge. No one seemed to know what it was. Finally the skipper called over the phone: "Bradley. Do your damned Geigers change the color of the water too?" I had no explanation, thinking that it must be suspended coral sand sucked up from the bottom, but feeling sure that no sand ever looked like that. Finally the engineer tuned in: "Lieutenant Lower, I believe that that green area is merely marking stain like they use on our life belts." This was a likely explanation. The stain could be used to mark the center of the explosion, or perhaps better to demonstrate the disturbance and displacement of the water by the shot and the falling geyser.

It was past time to be going in over the target, and after an exchange of salutations Commander Pew's ship left us and began climbing to the prearranged altitude. He was soon lost in the tufted strato-cumulus over the lagoon. Communications, however, were good, and at once we began to pick up their messages: "Sadeyes, this is Applejack One. Legs one and two completed. Zero dose legs one and two." They had found nothing in the atmosphere. Then we heard: "Leg four completed. Brief dose on leg four." After that, it was clear that Lars and Tom were getting into radiation over the center of the fleet even at that altitude. Indeed at one point they interrupted their broadcast to Sadeyes in order to advise us to make our first survey a thousand feet above the prearranged level.

This we did and soon confirmed the radioactivity found by Lars and Tom. The pattern was one of radiation coming up from the ships and from the water. At a thousand feet lower there was a considerable increase in the dosage. Starting down a leg we would get just the usual irregular click — click, click — click of "background" over our Geiger earphones. Then suddenly there would be a burst of clicks, a crescendo, merging into the high-toned screaming of increasing radioactivity. The needle of one Geiger counter would rapidly go off scale; then the next, set to a less sensitive range, would follow suit. Charlie Wells and I would excitedly nudge each other, mumble and blink to one another through the gas masks and try to keep pace with the rapidly changing levels of radiation. Knowing our position over the target, it was possible to decide whether or not we could safely continue our leg. And then, just as suddenly, the screaming would die in our ears, the needles waver and return to normal, and we would be across the reef of radiation.

It always seemed a little strange to me that at such a time the pilot should be calmly looking down at the fleet, or glancing over his instrument panel. And his navigator would be there, standing between the pilots, calmly directing our course, timing the legs, and indicating when the turns should be made. Something was wrong. We should be able to feel this barrage of gamma rays tearing through our bodies. It was there. It was hot.

We made only two flights. Lars and Tom a thousand feet lower were running into trouble — trouble in the form of radioactivity so intense as to be safe for only a few minutes. Finally we caught the message: "Abandoning leg four. Radiation . . . on leg four. Turning away upwind and standing by for further orders."

Lieutenant Lower looked around from his seat with a sort of half grin. "Did you get that?" he indicated with a nod.

"Sure. That's probably something between ten and twenty roentgens a day, Skipper."

"So what do we do? Break out the lead jeans?"

"No, that's not really so bad; you could stay around there for fifteen minutes."

"Thanks — but who's to write that letter to me dear old mither?"

"Oh, they'll send her an iron cross, Skip. You'll be a hero. She'll be awful proud of you."

"Yeah. Well. I haven't got a mither — so to hell with that."

Sadeyes soon wired back to both of us to discontinue our surveys. We were thankful for that. It is not that we were in any immediate danger. But with radiation so intense at such an altitude, that at water level would certainly be lethal. And this wasn't just a point source, it was spread out over an area miles square.

By noon it was clear that our beautiful lady, the *Sara*, was in a bad way and would probably not see another sunrise. We soon had a message from Sadeyes to get some low level photographs of her. No one liked that job, because she evidently had a supply of torpedoes on deck. She was a complete derelict. Her flight deck was littered with wreckage. A stump of the island was there; the rest had been blown away. Bow and stern she was slowly filling up and beginning to list to port.

Few ships in that anachronistic fleet would be missed, but the grand old lady was special. She should rightly be afloat in some Navy Yard with the *Constitution*. She belonged to an era of unrivaled American vigor. So many of her gallant sister ships and their able-bodied crews had gone to obscure, deep-water graves, we hated to see the *Sara* get hers like any ordinary fish in this atomic barrel.

By midafternoon relief planes arrived and we could head back for Kwaj. At evening the relief ships returned with the news that the *Sara* had finally gone down, her great hull barely covered in the shallow lagoon.

Friday, July 26, Baker plus one

Back to Bikini with the dawn. The live fleet is now anchored at the entrance to the atoll next to Enyu Island.

Sadeyes was waiting for us with orders to drag the entire atoll. This we did at whitecap and palm-frond level, following the surf from island to sandspit to island around the coral ring. It was a beautiful morning, clear and calm. Birds rose in flocks all about us, veering off in panic as we brushed over their rookeries. And the white sands and concentric colors of the coral reefs looked like agate against the still blue of the ocean. Radiation, however, was not to be found except over the target fleet, and up on the islands to the north.

We did, however, discover an area of rather intense radioactivity several miles to the north of the atoll. At first I couldn't understand it. We were miles from the fleet, flying over open water. Suddenly the Geiger tubes jammed and Bogart, who was flying with me today, jumped as though he'd been hooked up to one by the seat of his pants. We found ourselves passing over an oil slick, which, though miles from the island, must have come from the target fleet, having passed during the night over the reef between Amen Island and Bikini Island. Crisscrossing it several times we found it to be well over a mile long and nearly as wide.

We also made several surveys at different altitudes over the target fleet. Some of the ships were beginning to show internal injuries. The hulking *Nagato* had developed a list, and the *New York* carried her stern half underwater. The radioactivity had died away remarkably during the night, so that low altitude flying proved to be reasonably safe. This decline was to be expected; many of the fission products have short half lives, fading away in a few moments or hours. Roughly the radiation died away according to the formula $r = \frac{1}{\text{time}}$. The drop, precipitous at first, levels off just as rapidly and then we are stuck with the long actors.

Our air assignment is about over. The crude measurements of intensity are no longer necessary, and the next phase — that of making precise surveys of the ships, water, fish, coral — begins.

Saturday, July 27

At 2:30 this afternoon word came from Kwajalein that we should be ready to leave Ebeye by 3:00.

Monday, July 29

Ah, Ebeye; the Elysian sands and soft, sparkling days of Ebeye and Patrol Squadron 32! Going back to the U.S.S. *Haven*, in the hurricane center of this task force, seems like the second evacuation of the Garden of Eden. The confusion aboard this ship is indescribable. The gangways swarm with the monitors of the Radiological Safety Section heavily laden with gear, sweating and irate; the laboratories are filled with queer stenches and flickering lights; stacks of secret and dangerous information pile up in the corridors. We appear to have struck it rich. It is an interesting operation. I suppose this is the first major offensive ever conducted by a fleet while anchored snugly in a harbor. The main objective, of course, is to get the target ships underway once more as soon as possible. The Navy seems confident that this will not be long.

However, the danger is here. The Bomb did not explode and vanish as did its four predecessors; it is here everywhere. Only very limited operations can yet be conducted aboard the ships. Many are not safe for boarding at all. All sorties must be accompanied by a Geiger man, who with the help of his instruments decides whether an area, a ship, or a particular job is safe. He may allow only a few minutes before insisting that the spot be evacuated.

My particular sector on this changing front is most routine. It is in the "water counting" laboratories. Here we receive hundreds and hundreds of samples of water taken from different parts of the lagoon and from different depths. We run these into specially designed pigs of lead in which a Geiger chamber has been mounted. Counting the clicks per minute is done by means of an automatic "scaler" and the results are plotted on a map of the lagoon and target array. It gives a day-to-day picture of the movement of water and tells whether or not our live fleet is lying at anchor in dangerous water.

Such indeed proved to be the case this afternoon. We had found by repeated measurements that the water was steadily increasing in radioactivity, owing presumably to an up-welling of material from the bottom. By noon the intensity was such as to endanger our water intakes and evaporators, and so at the request of the Radiological Safety Section the entire live fleet up-anchored and sailed to a point nearer Enyu channel.

So far only four ships have been reported as sunk. The crew who went aboard the Jap cruiser *Sakawa* had an exciting time. That was on Baker Day. The *Sakawa* was clearly taking in water, and the plan was to try to beach her on Enyu. However, the old Chief in charge did not like the look of her as they approached, and much less the feel of her once aboard. He got worried. "I don't like it; something's wrong with the —— —— ship. She's a dead ship." At once he recalled all his men to their small boats. They had not much more than cleared the stern when the *Sakawa* slowly rolled over, up-ended, and sank hissing to the bottom.

Wednesday, July 31

Last night the *Nagato* disappeared into its shallow grave. For days she had been listing and apparently leaking from numerous seams, although she was reported to be the most unsinkable ship in the fleet. For all her double hull and intricate compartmentation, she proved to be obsolete in close quarters with the Bomb. She was close in to the Bomb, which, having its force confined by water and the shallow bottom of the lagoon, must have developed a fantastically powerful upward thrust, against which modern hulls and compartmentation are of no avail. (This same effect of confining and concentrating the power of a bomb would be the case were a bomb to explode down some metropolitan slot like Wall Street.)

I, for one, am not sorry to see the *Nagato* gone. She was a massive and brutal structure, having neither grace nor beauty. She gave no comforting illusion that war is anything but an ugly, brutal, and totally insane preoccupation of man.

Friday, August 2

The work of the task force does not become easier with succeeding days. The skeleton crews of the target ships have been anxiously awaiting the signal to start the motors and get steam up. But so far most of the ships are still in quarantine because of radioactivity. Work in most instances is permissible below decks, but without the blowers on and the lights functioning there is little to be done but keep the ships pumped out. Some, like the *New York*, have to be pumped steadily. Topsides these target ships are still so hot as to permit only short shifts of twenty minutes to an hour. The rain which fell contained the equivalent of tons of radium. Naturally the Navy has complete faith in the old ritual of "a clean sweep-down fore and aft," but to date little seems to be accomplished by repeated scrubbings.

Tugs equipped with fire-fighting apparatus are engaged in most spectacular hydraulic procedures. Salt water and foamite have streaked the vessels, giving them a cadaverous appearance, but no relief from the "damned Geigers." Fission products, having fallen like a coat of paint over these ships, cannot be washed off by salt water and suds.

Saturday, August 3

Most of the radioactivity dispersed in the water seems to have settled out. At least it is no longer necessary to do samples of lagoon water. The water counting lab has therefore nearly gone out of business in favor of the more strenuous ship-monitoring jobs. We continue to check the ships' evaporators and water lines so that faulty distillation will not be letting radioactive material through into the drinking water.

The evaporators aboard the U.S.S. *Haven* have become quite hot in themselves, the scale inside the evap tanks acting as a sponge for radioactive particles. Similarly the salt-water lines of the ship (fire lines, toilets, and so on) show the presence of radioactivity too, and must be checked every day or two. A third area of radioactive infection aboard the ship is the green and brown algae which grow along the waterlines. The algae especially have become hot from the fission products picked up during the first days following our return to Bikini. For some reason or other the algae do not release their radioactivity and so the water lines remain so hot that one may pick up a respectable radiation coming through the steel walls of the hull.

The presence of radioactive material on and within the ships of the live fleet suggests an interesting complication: what will happen when the ships are dry-docked for repairs? Will it be safe for workmen to remove the scale from the evaps, and the barnacles from the hulls? Will such tasks in the future have to be done with gas masks or oxygen rebreathers, and all the material collected and buried at sea?

To such questions theoretical answers are easy; practical ones are much harder. But in the end the Navy, in asking for this closer acquaintance with atomic energy, is going to feel a lot like Br'er Rabbit when he got mixed up with the Tar Baby; they may not know it yet, but they are stuck with it.

The whole business must seem like a very bad dream to the regular Navy men: decks you can't stay on for more than a few minutes but which seem like other decks; air you can't breathe without gas masks but which smells like all other air; water you can't swim in, and good tuna and jacks you can't eat. It's a fouled-up world. And now the docs are measuring the evaporators and water mains, and saying that the ships will be too dangerous to haul out in dry dock! Damned Geigers and Geiger men!

I've often wondered what the Navy men thought

when they came upon some mysterious figure, decked out in galoshes, gloves, coveralls, and mask, creeping along the passages of an able-bodied ship, waving a magic black box over the water pipes and listening intently through earphones as though tuned in on the supernatural. They must feel that the good old Navy is being taken over by screwballs.

Sunday, August 4

Today, a trip ashore with a group from the U.S. Fisheries and from the Museum of Natural History. They were interested in seeing what effect, if any, the presence of radioactivity had had upon marine and island life. Three islands and the intervening reef have had a heavy exposure. The great oil slick heavily impregnated with fission products, which formed about the target ships on Baker Day, apparently swept over the reef at this point and on out into the sea where on Baker plus one we discovered it several miles to the north of Bikini Island. Like a slow neutron in a pile this floating island was attracted back to the atoll and has come ashore all along our northeastern flank. The shore line and sandspits are here smeared over with the gummy emulsion which may take years to leach away. Considering this and the fact that the coral and fish have become radioactive to an alarming degree, it is doubtful if the Bikini natives will be able to return to their wrecked island for years to come.

Our work out on the reef was not far removed from youth's ecstasy of exploration. Several of the men were collecting samples of coral, algae, and various weeds in areas exposed to radiation. None of these areas proved to be so hot that a person could not remain in them for at least one hour, and there was no change immediately evident in the specimens as a result of their exposure. We saw no dead or dying fish, such as were rumored to be lying along the shore, but none of us expected to find any. In the first place this is almost too soon for radioactivity to be killing fish. The slow dissolution of their vital organs resulting from the unrelenting rays may take weeks or months to kill. And secondly, one almost never sees a dying fish under any circumstances in these waters. Whenever a fish gets so sick and logy that his reflexes for self-preservation are slowed down a fraction of a second, he is snapped up by his predatory brethren. Therefore, short of an accurate, broad population study of fish before and after the Baker test it will be very hard to estimate the effect of an atomic bomb on fish.

It was a beautiful day out on the reef, with the long seas breaking over the purple barrier. Schools of jeweled fish swam in and out of the crevasses, and occasionally the small suede-coated sand sharks would come circling around to see what was happening.

Not so long ago Bikini must have been a beautiful island. It still has areas of palm and pandanus and bread-

fruit where all is peace and sunshine and the whispering
of the trades. The hot sand, littered with shells and bits
of crimson coral, the grass and dense undergrowth, the
sparkle of the lagoon, and the booming of the surf on
the reef give one the impression of complete timeless-
ness. There is an uninterrupted continuity and harmony
of nature which does not seem to belong to the same
old world we come from. No lotus grows here, none
is necessary; there is nothing to remember and therefore
nothing to forget.

Of the original native village little remains but a few
thatched frames which once were houses. The Seabees
live here now, having swept the area almost clean of
vegetation with bulldozers and churned it into dust with
their trucks. After our work was done, we stopped in at
the Seabee Club and pried them loose from a case of
beer. Then we sat in the shade of some coconut palms
eating lunch, watching the dark ships, and the boatloads
of sailors coming ashore, and giving ourselves over to
the process of osmosis.

Friday, August 9

A second trip with the U.S. Fisheries group. Today
we went dredging in the center of the target area for
samples of the bottom. Shallow-water diving men have
recently reported areas where the coral heads have been
bleached out white, the animals which give such rich
hues of red and purple to their crusty domiciles being

dead. Whether this can be considered the result of excessive radiation, rather than some other factor like gasoline and oil, cannot be conclusively proved, but if the radiation at the bottom of the lagoon is any fair test it is not an unreasonable assumption. Our first netful of sand dumped upon the fantail of our boat proved to be so radioactive that in a panic I had the whole catch thrown overboard.

But the look on the face of my good friend Dr. Taylor of Woods Hole was too much. This lean, tireless scientist saw us destroying a beautiful catch of unusual specimens for which he had traveled ten thousand miles. And so on the succeeding catches we agreed to save small samples which would then be kept in properly leaded boxes and studied only by him.

I think none of us expected the bottom to show such intensities at this late date. It poses the interesting question of whether or not the fish which live by browsing on coral and algae may ultimately be destroyed by the collection of radioactive materials within their bodies. And if so, then what will become of the larger fish which live off of the smaller fish; will they too become infected and pass on the plague of radioactivity? That is a study which would occupy at least a year out here.

In the afternoon I was assigned to make a survey of the *New York*. This venerable old battlewagon, constructed about 1912, was pretty badly hit. Her superstructures aft are a jungle of steel, and she has been taking in water enough in the stern to require almost continuous pumping. There is no thought any more of getting steam up on her. Radioactive material has leaked into her after compartments, and has come in through every portal and companionway above. Stores of food, hundreds of pounds of coffee, and even the drinking water have had to be condemned.

The work of the day, however, was decontamination. All previous attempts have been notably unsuccessful. The decks have been sluiced down with water. When this caused no reduction in radioactivity buckets of soap were broken out. Still the same result. The magic formula of a "clean sweep-down fore and aft" is out of date in the atomic age.

Today a trial was being made of alkali. The main deck forward had not been touched as yet and here we proposed to run the experiment. I made a careful survey of the deck, finding the intensity to vary a great deal in a matter of feet. One gets the impression that fission products have become most fixed in the tarry calking of the planking and in rusty spots in the metal plates.

When the survey was complete the Chief turned his booted, sweating, profane, and laughing crew loose with brushes, water, and a barrel of lye. Yet when the hydraulics were done and the deck rinsed clean again, another survey showed the invisible emanations to be present doing business as usual. The portly Chief stood watching the dial of my Geiger counter, completely bewildered. The deck was clean, anybody could see that, clean enough for the Admiral himself to eat his breakfast off of. So what was all this goddam radioactivity? Finally he could stand it no longer:

"Here, Doc, let me listen to that gadget, will you?"

I fitted the headphones over his ears. He stood moving the gadget over the deck as I had done and, listening intently, he shook his head:

"Must be fouled up. I only get static now . . ."

"That's all you ever get, Chief. What did you expect, Dorothy Lamour?"

He looked dubious: "Well, what are they, them clicks? Do they mean anything?"

"They sure do, Chief. Each of those clicks is a little bullet shooting through your body. You get enough of them and they will kill you. You don't know it but this deck is a booby trap."

Still unconvinced but taken with the gadget he went off for a cruise around his deck. He'd seen two wars fought out from that deck. He wasn't particularly concerned about a stray bullet or two. Finally he hove to beside a stanchion where several of his men were resting themselves. They grinned at him as he surveyed the area. Then suddenly he straightened up:

"Here, you guys," he said with gruff authority, "get the hell off that stanchion. Can't you see you're sittin' on a goddam booby trap?"

The sailors took off from that stanchion as though

440 volts had hit them, dusting off their jeans, and feeling behind as though they expected to find something sticking there. Feeling nothing they laughed:

"Ahhhh, it don't matter, Chief," kidded one of them, "I got so many of them Geigers runnin' round inside me now that you can see me all lit up at night like the Statue of Liberty."

"That's right," added another. "Since I been out here I've grown seventy years old. I don't care if I don't never see another woman. I'm a goner. I'm hopeless."

The Chief had been right. Where the stanchion was fastened to the deck there was a good deal of tar, and this had picked up quantities of the invisible stuff. When I showed this to the detail and let them listen to the earphones, they appeared to believe either that I was just another old woman dressed up as a medical officer asking them to wear their rubbers out in the rain, or that they were all doomed to complete and rapid dissolution. They were not quite sure which.

So I told them a little about radiation sickness, in experimental animals and what I knew of the people of Hiroshima, what the dangerous levels of intensity were and what we were trying to do to protect them from exposure.

Finally one young kid — he couldn't have been over eighteen — serious, shy, and hopefully unshaven, piped up:

"Doc," he asked, "what about the six fellows? Was it the Geigers that got them?"

It wasn't the first time I had heard the rumor. Many another sailor had reported the same story. "What fellows do you mean?"

"Oh, I don't know 'em. Only we heard that six guys had already kicked in out here."

"Well, I know of a couple who died of drinking wood alcohol, but so far as I know no one has been killed or even injured by radiation out here. You probably are thinking about the men who were killed at Los Alamos. I know of two personally, one who got involved in an accidental explosion just before we came out here. But they were well-trained scientists working with extremely dangerous stuff. What we have spread out over twenty-five miles, they were working with in one room. See?"

"Well, if nobody is getting hurt, Doc, why do we bother with all this damn scrubbin'?" The old Chief was still trying to figure out what was happening to his Navy. "Why don't we just get steam up on these buckets and haul out of here before we rot and sink at our chains?"

"I'll tell you, Chief. It is because even this amount of stuff is dangerous. For two reasons: first, it doesn't take much to kill you. If this stuff were all radium and you got a piece no bigger than a grain of salt inside you, you'd be a goner. Fortunately, most of the fission products aren't quite that bad — or we'd all be goners by now. And the second reason why we are so darned careful is that there is a lot of stuff out here we don't know about, stuff that can't be picked up on a Geiger machine. Some of that material is plenty dangerous."

The detail was having its first and probably its last lesson in radiology. They were puzzled, and it was hard to make them understand. "Most of the fission products are quite insoluble. They won't be absorbed into your body even though you breathe them in or get them into your mouth. So from them you only have to worry about radiation coming in from the outside — and that we can control with a Geiger machine. But some of the material — like plutonium remaining from the Bomb — is dangerous, more dangerous than radium even. Like the rest of the stuff it is spread around here like a thin coat of paint and can't be washed off. So, although we cannot detect it specifically, if we pick up other radiations on our Geiger counters we have fair warning that the more dangerous substances may be around too."

"And what happens when that little box gets snafued?" returned the boy who had recently been dusting off the stanchion.

"That is where the film badges come in. You all wear them in your pockets. The film is exposed just like X-ray film and we can tell how much you've been getting."

The fallacy of such a protective measure was obvious to them at once: "Sure, but that only tells you afterwards. A lot of good that is when you've been fried all day in X rays."

That was wonderful — to have them understand the problem so well as to be able to reason with it. I said: "You're right. That's just it. And that is why we have been so conservative. The task force has accepted a certain limit of radiation as safe. But that limit is not the fatal one. It gives you almost a thousandfold safety factor. By that I mean you could probably take a thousand times that limit at one time and not be killed. And that is okay for peacetime maneuvers. It wouldn't work for war. If this ship had been hit by an atom bomb during a battle — or if this were some big city back home — we would all have to get in there and do what we could with the situation and take our chances on being killed now or later with Geigers, the same as with fire and smoke and shells."

Baker Day, Bikini Atoll, 1946. The fireball is just erupting from the lagoon, 185 feet deep . . .

. . . as 10,000,000 tons of water, mud, coral sand, and steam are mixed in a brew of fission products.

The chimney is half a mile across and two miles high. The black hole carved on the right was the last naval act of the battleship *Arkansas*.

Little of the fallout escapes into the atmosphere. The fleet receives a coat of radioactive paint.

THE COUNT OF TEN

Saturday, August 10, 1946

Today the great change, which for a week has been going through the labor pains of rumor, was born as established policy: Operation Crossroads as an experiment is being abandoned. A skeleton task force will remain out here to keep the target vessels afloat, and a skeleton Radiological Safety Section will stay to carry on the public health work. Volunteers are being rounded up for the job. Most of the trained scientific personnel, being civilian and pressed with teaching and research engagements stateside, will have to leave, and so of course will the higher echelon of Navy personnel. The formidable cruisers, the destroyers, and the sleek carriers will soon be gone, ringing down the curtain on all the pomp and pageantry of Operation Crossroads.

Things have not gone according to plan. The target fleet which was to have steamed triumphantly back to Pearl and the Golden Gate, invincible as ever, will remain here at anchor, blackened with flame and streaked with foamite and rust, until the ships can be safely disposed of. Some may eventually be towed to the West

Coast; many will certainly be sunk in deep water.

A few ships, notably the submarines, have been given clearance to go to Pearl Harbor for repairs and further decontamination, but the rest remain. Some inkling of the danger which persists aboard these ships can be gleaned from the conditions imposed by the Admiral on all future operations: (1) that all work will be done as before under the direct supervision of the Radiological Safety Section, with 1/10 of a roentgen still the maximum daily dose permitted, and (2) that all work henceforth will be confined to that necessary for closing up the ships.

This is a momentous decision, a momentous admission. By some it was anticipated, knowing the nature of the disease of radioactivity. By many others it will be welcomed as an awakening from a very bad dream, a chance to get stateside duty, or at least to get back to the good old regular Navy where the world behaves according to Newtonian physics and a "clean sweep-down" can be counted on to work.

There are many reasons behind this decision. Among those which are not secret are (1) that these ships are fouled up with radioactivity to a degree far greater than anticipated, (2) that this coat of radioactive paint cannot be scrubbed off or removed by any of the ordinary measures, short of chipping off all the paint and rust, and uprooting all the planking from the outsides of the ships, (3) and that there is a real hazard from elements present which cannot be detected by the ordinary field methods.

The degree of efficiency of the Bomb is top secret, but recent studies with the alpha counter have established the presence of alpha emitters, notably plutonium. These studies include samples of paint from ships' decks, samples of rust, and even air samples taken from within ships by means of a vacuum cleaner device and filter paper.

These are probably some of the reasons why the care of the target vessels has become ultraconservative, and why the time schedule for Operation Crossroads has had to be scrapped. I have no regrets that this great fleet of once able-bodied ships, once rich in the vaingloriousness of military traditions, has come to this end. Men are more important than the ships they build, and this fleet might instead be my own home town. From a military point of view the Bomb which wreaked havoc in Hiroshima also knocked out Task Force One. We've just come to the count of ten.

The state of flux which exists throughout the task force at this moment has finally descended upon the sanctum sanctorum of science. Orders have come that the water counting lab will change its name to Urinalysis Lab and prepare to study the urines of all exposed men. To me this was the cruelest cut of all.

We began the metamorphosis today by testing urine samples from monitors of the Radiological Safety Section, who have probably had more constant exposure than any other group. Some of them showed pretty high counts and gave us all, especially the monitors in question, a fair state of jitters. But after checking our instruments and our technique, we are right back to the old dilemma: are we getting evidence of radioactivity, or are we merely recording the statistical variation possible in the instrument? Grover Carter and Rex Huff have begun careful research into the problem of what the limit of reliability of our instruments is, and what would be the most exact method for determining radioactivity in urine samples.

Today the monitors — a couple of score of them. Tomorrow the levee begins to sag, and after that the whole business caves in and we shall be inundated with hundreds and hundreds of bottles of urine from the crews of the *New York*, *Salt Lake City*, *Pensacola*, *Prinz Eugen*, and so on.

Thursday, August 15

Urinalysis: Over 1200 samples to date.

Result: No definite evidence of radioactivity present.

Conclusions: The law of diminishing return is out of date in the atomic age. The schedule now calls for 2500.

The great task force of Operation Crossroads has fizzed (verb coined by scientists from noun "fission"; alternative pronunciation is "fished"). It is breaking up into many smaller sections and spreading out in all directions. After tomorrow only a small group will remain. Those who are escaping from this lagoon of horrors have become a little euphoric. Great things, they feel, have been done out here for science and humanity and great things could still be done.

One of our most blissful optimists is a captain in the Air Corps, an entomologist by training. In his youth he studied cockroaches, and this passion he followed throughout the war in the ample laboratory resources of Army life. Well, one day this gentleman was prowling around the battleship *New York*, ostensibly monitoring below decks but actually looking to see if there might be something to eat. He found the larder and what is more he noticed that a large clan of cockroaches had moved in ahead of him. Finding that most of the food was contaminated with radioactive material — probably brought in on the shoes of sailors who had had the same idea weeks earlier — he was suddenly struck with the light. Cockroaches and food, radioactive food! Would they survive? How much could they eat? Would it affect their reproductive powers? So our friend collected a boxful of cockroaches, brought them back to the *Haven*, and carefully stowed them in his gear for study when he got back to the United States. I have often wondered what his home life will be like when he arrives and his wife, asking for a souvenir of Bikini, is rewarded with a box of radioactive cockroaches.

Another of our homing scientists came in with a report that the rats on a certain ship were looking pretty sick. It was his recommendation that the laboratory collect a large group of rats, dead or live, and study the effects of radiation on them. He wrote a monograph on the subject of radioactivity in rats, and the idea sounded so good to those in authority that one of our lieutenants, Medical Corps, was detailed to the project. The only item which the monograph failed to advise on was how to catch rats. The lieutenant set out his traps and left enough poison around to kill off the entire ship's seagoing complement, and then hopefully waited for the rats to come staggering in. Only they never came, and if they died at all it was from laughing themselves to death.

The experiment came to an appropriate conclusion today when, by accident, the lieutenant got left aboard the hot ship all alone. No one knew he was there, his boatman having forgotten all about him. He couldn't go on deck for very long because it was too radioactive. And he didn't know how to run the radio. By sunset-time, unwilling to face a night in a ship overrun with rats alive or spectral, he was contemplating the long swim back to the *Haven*, sharks or no sharks, when by good luck he was spotted by a fish-collecting expedition and rescued.

Friday, August 16

To the east, to Pearl and America; to the west, to China and Japan. The lagoon of Bikini, once a city of light, looks strangely barren. The dark and silent ships await their final disposal. A few seagoing tugs and gunboats remain with the *Haven*. All is quiet aboard and ashore. This is still Operation Crossroads, only now the crossroads has a large psychological sign placed across it: DETOUR. DANGER AHEAD!

Tuesday, August 20

Urinalysis: Approaching 3000 mark.

Findings: No definite evidence of radioactivity.

Conclusions: Well, let's see.

What can you conclude from three thousand urine samples, taken from crews who have since Baker plus one been off and on aboard the hottest target ships? First you have to decide what are the limits of accuracy of your measurements and the factors which govern those limits.

The first factor is the accuracy of your instruments and the method of counting. Unfortunately out here we have only the instruments previously used for water counting for our urinalysis. In the early days following the Baker shot they were used to analyze lagoon water which was intensely radioactive. They naturally became "contaminated" by material which coated the tubes and lead pigs exactly as it coated the ships. This means that each counter has a high "background count." The normal statistical variation of the counter occurring purely on the basis of chance during any particular run will, therefore, be great. This variation will be in inverse proportion to the length of time the sample is counted. One could probably eliminate the chance variation by counting each sample for a week, but at that rate even Methuselah would be on old age pension before the task force survey was done.

In the Manhattan District it has been the practice to use nothing but new instruments, new pipettes, new glassware, and so on, for studies which require accuracy. They think nothing of junking a whole laboratory with all its equipment when a significant amount of contamination is present. And it is their practice to regard six counts per minute above background in a man's urine as significant. We cannot hope for any such accuracy out here.

A second variable is the time when the urine was collected. If a man has fission products inside his body, taken in his mouth or lungs, much of it will not be absorbed at all. Of that which is absorbed, part will be permanently fixed in the tissues, and the rest will be excreted. Excretion, however, is not an even process. Probably by far the great majority of what is to be excreted will come out in the first 24 hours. This means that the most reliable measure of fission products contained within the body will be found in the excretion which immediately follows the exposure.

In the third place one can never be sure that a particular sample which gives a reading above background really represents the exposure of the patient. Contamination of the sample is too easy. Fresh bottles can be fouled up by material from the hands of the person giving the sample, and from equipment used in its analysis.

It is evident, therefore, that at best our urinalysis is a crude and scarcely scientific procedure. Yet it is the best we can do under the limitations of our equipment and our method. It is always possible to check suspicious samples by evaporating and ashing down large volumes of urine and counting them for longer times in cleaner instruments — and this is done, but it too is a method subject to similar limitations.

A fourth variable enters into any attempt to interpret a finding of radioactivity in urine. Fission products contain a multiplicity of radioactive elements, each with its own properties. Some may be so insoluble as never to be absorbed. Others may be absorbed and fixed within the body, giving no sign of their presence thereafter. Some may be quite harmless in small amounts owing to a rapid rate of decay; others may be toxic chemically or dangerous in very small quantities owing to their special radioactivity.

It must be evident, therefore, that one must interpret urinalyses within their proper context. The conditions mentioned are not remote conjecture, they are the conditions we have to face here with the explosion of the fifth atomic bomb. And they are conditions, if less favorable than those of the Manhattan District laboratories, which are still far better than one could hope for in a time of atomic war. Indeed it is hard to imagine that a population or an army exposed to a similar rain of radioactive material could ever afford the luxury of urinalysis. From a medical as well as from a military point of view, urinalysis, blood counts, and other such protective measures would be about as useful to a fellow in such a catastrophe as Metropolitan Life Insurance.

Our urinalysis procedures, however, have not been wholly wasted. If nothing else, they have given conviction to our concern over radioactivity. The practical and rather sceptical men of the Navy have ceased to regard the Radiological Safety Section as a society of cranky old maids. "Radiation is spooky business, but if the docs are willing to go to such limits to protect the task force there must be something in it after all."

As a matter of fact lately we have been getting volunteer samples from jittery individuals who have never been aboard target ships. Today a deputation came from the Seabee contingent on the island. Their only conceivable exposure was from working and swimming along the shore, which for weeks has shown no significant activity. Nevertheless they had been at Operation Crossroads, and if urinalyses were in order they were not to be left out.

Thursday, August 22

With the discovery, by divers, that areas of coral were bleaching out into chalky white from some unexplainable and lethal agent has come an increasing concern over the fish. Small reef fish feed on coral and algae among the heads, and have been picking up considerable quantities of the material and storing it in various parts of their bodies, notably the gills, the liver, the intestines, and in the organs of reproduction. Some of the men down in X ray have demonstrated this most dramatically by means of "radio-autographs" of the entire fish.

These radio-autographs are made by taking a small fish, slicing it longitudinally down the middle, drying it in a blast of warm air, and then placing the fish, cut side down, on a photographic plate. After a suitable time the radioactivity present in the tissues of the fish will have exposed the adjacent film, which, when developed, will then outline the fish in tones which are proportional to the radioactivity present. We have several of them. They demonstrate clearly the pattern of selective absorption of fission products by the various tissues. One can see the gills darkly outlined, the long coiled intestine, the large burst of radioactivity associated with the liver, and the less dark areas of the gonads. The rest of the fish, muscle, bone, scales, shows only a trace of the material. This is hard on the fish but a most fortunate thing for man, since not a few fish have been eaten by careless or optimistic Waltonians out here.

What is true of the reef fish now will become increasingly true of the larger migratory fish — the tuna, the jacks, the sharks, and so on — as the latter, the predatory fish, eat more and more of the smaller fish who are sick with the disease of radioactivity. We know that this process is going on. Almost all seagoing fish recently caught around the atoll of Bikini have been radioactive. Thus the disease is passed on from species to species like an epizootic. The only factors which tend to limit the disease, as distinguished from infectious diseases, are the half lives of the materials involved, and the degree of dilution and dissemination of the fission products.

What the immediate results of this situation will be cannot be predicted. I believe that there is enough radioactivity present at the bottom of this lagoon to kill fish either by the total radiation to the body, or by the destruction of vital organs by absorbed radioactivity, but it would take a careful study of the fish population extending over many months to prove it. I doubt that the amount of radiation carried away by migratory fish to other parts of the Pacific will constitute any hazard either to fish or to man because of the great dilution factor. But whether we would be safe in that assumption in the event of an atomic war, with a large number of bombs exploding in coastal areas and seaports, is another question. Conceivably the fishing industry would be entirely wrecked, and the fish rendered unsafe for eating at a time when food of any kind was critically needed.

The gross and spectacular demonstration of radioactivity in fish by means of radio-autographs has to be supplemented by a more accurate study of the separate tissues, isolated, ashed down, and counted in a sensitive beta-gamma counter. This investigation has been one of the side-interests of the laboratory. Whenever possible we go on fishing trips to collect specimens. Such trips, however, depend much on the mood of the Executive Officer and the condition of his ulcer at the time. The Exec, for some reason, cannot regard these "Radiobiologic Collection Trips" as anything but thinly disguised fishing trips and afternoons off from the tedium of urinalysis.

Today was no exception. The weather being almost perfect for piscatorial pleasures, the Exec, having to remain on duty on the *Haven*, was in a particularly joyless mood. But there wasn't much he could do about it, since Commander Harris, our new chief of the Radiological Safety Section, had decided to take the afternoon off and go fishing with us. So we rigged our trolling gear, our hand lines, bottles of formalin, sharpened our spears, set off in an LCP(L) an hour or so before low tide. Amen Island was our hunting ground. Once there the group divided up, Commander Harris taking the boat to troll for tuna. Most of the others went to hand-lining for small fish off the pontoon wharf while Carter, an expert spear fisherman, and I took our arrows and slingshots and crossed the narrow sandy palm-encanopied island to the north side. Here the barrier reef is low and relatively abrupt, and the surf not impassable.

Reef fishing in such waters as these is less a sport than a form of art. It is a sudden emergence into an unimagined world of beauty and fantasy. But to fish on the oceanside of an atoll one has to pass the barrier of the inrolling surf. Frequently, when the tide is wrong or the waves high, this barrier is impassable, and to be caught out in the ragged shallow water where the waves come avalanching in would be like going over Niagara Falls in a barrel of razor blades. Today, however, the waves are low, and by standing just inside the reef, where they have lost their thrust, one soon comes to feel the rhythm of breaking and to see the larger waves far out before they begin to break. Then, when several large ones have passed and the way is finally clear, it takes but a quick dash, stumbling and half swimming, to bring one beyond the white zone into deeper water. It is a little like flight across a field of cabbages and broken glass on a dark night — but urgency guides your feet and holds your hand, and soon you are safe where the shelf sinks away into the black canyons of the Pacific. Here you may float above the weird and beautiful coral outcrops. The flux of water ebbing and flooding through the caverns cradles you in perfect safety. Here the small fish abound, and the spear fishing is good.

Actually we spear few fish because the turbulence of the water and the agility of the fish stack the cards all in their favor. But we get enough on which to make radiological observations and consider ourselves fortunate indeed just to be able to live a few moments in such a world.

The deeper draught fish seek the deeper water, and so the temptation is to go further and further out. There the fissures become gorges and the gorges vast canyons, while the coral rises around you in castellated outcrops, merging into hills, and at last into mountain ranges having summits but no bases.

Your tempter may be a large parrot fish, chunky, solemn, brilliantly turquoise in color; or perhaps one of those solitary mullets, built like an orange crate, who keep a ponderous and portly isolation.

I followed one such fish out into deep water today, a squirrelfish whose shapely body seemed to be encased in chain mail made of polished copper. He kept moving away in mild disinterest, sinking steadily into the dusk of the confluent canyons like some object pursued with the leaden steps of a dream. A shot was soon hopeless, but in the fascination of that dream I continued to follow him out over his mountainous empire until suddenly the dream changed to a chilly nightmare, as out of the ultramarine a massive gray shape began to emerge. Unmistakable, his identity: the head as big as an oil barrel, the pectoral fins like half crescents, the tapering body and whiplash tail. He half rolled once, to give me a good looking over, and I could see the pyramid of that gray dorsal fin. In thirty feet of water, and a hundred yards from surf, I had no chance to escape him. So like any sensible trespasser, I tried to move away as unobtrusively as possible. The shark effortlessly made a survey of his domain, and apparently satisfied by my feeble efforts to retreat, he slunk austerely away and disappeared.

After that the surf could hold few terrors. Carter was there, his feet thrashing in the foam while he made shot after shot at the fish. Underwater I could hear the clink of his arrows as they struck the coral. Carter has been our most intrepid swimmer. He seems to have no fear of surf. Several times he had been rolled by large waves, but inshore is where the fishing is best and so that is where Carter operates. He had several fish, among them a large parrot fish, and so in spite of his wounds was exultant over the catch.

After an hour or so even the tropical Pacific becomes chilly. By the time we returned to the pier Lars and Tom and the rest had caught a good mess of small fish and Commander Harris, though unable to persuade the particular tuna, had come back with a third degree sunburn on the top of his balding head. The day was declared a huge success, and save for running hard on a coral head, the trip back to the *Haven* and the silent decimated fleet was uneventful.

Analysis of the catch was interesting. Of the fish caught on the lagoon side of the reef, all showed considerable radioactivity; while those taken from the ocean side showed none. This would indicate that dissemination of radioactive material will be slow from Bikini's lagoon, and should allow time for a careful study of the effects of radiation of this sort on marine life over the course of weeks and months. It is a factor which bodes well for fishing industries in this general area, since the danger of contaminated fish being caught will be minimal.

Friday, August 23

Bogart, who flew lagoon reconnaissance with me on that faraway day, Baker plus one, came in today with the latest information on the decontamination of ships. Having proved at last, to their own satisfaction, that salt water, lye, foamite, soap, spread with liberal amounts of Navy profanity, have no value in cleaning these ships of their coat of radioactivity, the Navy has recently decided to try sandblasting. This has been Bogart's little assignment. It is tedious, hot work, and since there may be a danger from inhaled radioactive dust, it has to be carried on by men fully clothed and working in oxygen rebreathing apparatus. Next to a diver's suit, there is nothing more cumbersome and trying on the nerves than such a costume in the tropics.

It appears that sandblasting will remove radioactivity, that is to say, when all of the paint has been blasted off. Clearly this is no answer to the fleet's problem. You can't sandblast a whole ship under battle conditions. You can't sandblast Pearl Harbor, or Bremerton Shipyards, or Chicago. Possibly with great quantities of strong acid you may be able to remove enough paint to clear the decks of fission products. Lars has shown this in laboratory tests on strips of paint. But short of that the coat of radioactivity is on to stay. I can think of no fact demonstrated by the Bikini tests which is more important in its widest implications than this difficulty in ridding the habitable surfaces of our world of contaminating fission products.

Rex Huff performed a simple but revealing experiment the other day. He had been working with a crew of deck scrubbers. And when they, like the rest, found that no amount of lye and elbow grease was removing the radioactivity, Rex dug up a piece of wood from the deck. This he took to our carpenter shop, where he could plane strips from the surface, measuring the surface radioactivity after each planing. He found that he had to remove about a half centimeter — which is something less than a quarter of an inch — of the wood before he had removed all of the radioactivity. It was his conclusion that all the washing we were doing only served to soak the fission products more deeply and permanently into the wood.

If then we are faced with having to chip off all the paint and to plane off all the wooden surfaces of our contaminated ships the degree of disablement of ships by a water-bursting atomic bomb is ever so much more than was anticipated before the Baker test. Doubtless there will be other methods of meeting the problem.

Some of the more nimble-minded men of the Navy are suggesting that ships be painted with a plastic coat something like that which is now being used to protect the guns from weathering — a coat which, when contaminated to a dangerous degree, may be stripped off the ship in sheets and thrown overboard. But even if this could be made practical for ships, how would we yet be able to take care of our cities with their brick buildings and cement sidewalks?

Saturday, August 24

We have had few medical emergencies out here. Considering how many seamen have been at work on these ships, encumbered by oxygen rebreathing apparatus and heavy clothing, working in dark gangways and on hopelessly wrecked decks, it is remarkable that there have not been more emergencies. Today we had our first serious radiation problem. Carter, Huff, and I were working on a better process for urinalysis when a corpsman suddenly appeared.

"Sir, there's an emergency in surgery. Dr. Williams would very much like someone to come down."

"Okay. Sure. What's the hitch?"

"Some sailor got cut with a cable and he thinks he's full of them Geigers, sir."

That was bad news. We ran down to the instrument room to get a counter, and then followed the corpsman down to the operating theater. The sailor, a husky fellow in his late teens, was lying on the operating table beneath the glare of the overhead lights. He was in no particular pain, but pale and sweating from fright. Two Navy doctors, gowned, gloved and masked, were washing out his wound with sterile solution. It was not much more than a superficial laceration of the base of the thumb, and fortunately was still bleeding well.

Dr. Williams was obviously relieved to see us. "Brad, this man got hurt on some cable aboard one of the target ships. It doesn't look too bad — but I don't know what to do with it."

The sailor told us the name of the ship; it was one of the beached vessels and was moderately contaminated on deck. "We was trying to get her clear for the trip to Kwaj. I was heaving in on one of the cables when it broke and tore my hand. Don't seem too bad, but one of the Geiger men was there and he sent me right over here."

"Did he examine the cable?"

"Yes, sir. It had been in the water, and he said it was radioactive."

My thoughts went back to the Manhattan Project. There, in laboratories and plants where people are working with purified plutonium there is a policy which requires immediate high amputation for anyone in a similar situation. The metal is rapidly absorbed from cuts and lacerations, and once within the body it is quickly fixed in the marrow part of the bones, where, like radium, it may be lethal in fantastically small amounts.

The situation is a little different here. Most of the fission products are quite insoluble and will not be absorbed nearly so rapidly if at all. Plutonium is known to be present, but in small amounts. Knowing as little as we actually do of the various elements present on these decks, I hated to be responsible for an unnecessary amputation; yet an error on the other side would be worse.

I hesitated, and Dr. Williams, reading my thoughts, said:

"I told him that he might have to have an amputation."

At this, the sailor closed his eyes but said nothing.

"Well, maybe, and maybe not," I said to him. "You understand, though, that if you got a lot of hot stuff into your hand from that cable your best chance is to have your arm off."

He nodded. "Sure. That's what the Geiger man said too. You're the doctor."

We looked his hand over carefully, setting the Geiger tube right down on the wound. There was no count, so then Dr. Williams injected a novocaine block and débrided the edges of the wound. As these bits of tissue, dried on filter paper, also gave no reading we felt confident that the wound was not seriously contaminated and could be safely closed without amputation. There was never a boy more thankful to be "returned to duty" than that sailor, nor a doctor more thankful to be out of an operation.

Sunday, August 25, Baker plus one month

Another sparkling day, with all the ecstatic brilliance which heralds the end of summer, even in the tropics — the lagoon glittering darkly with its squally winds, and the ships standing all about us, within the dark fringe of palms, gray and gaunt, yawing restlessly at their moorings. The air has the smell, and the sea and sky the look, of October — one of those intense days which suddenly come to wake up a somnolent summer and announce that fall is taking over. Such has been our last day at Bikini.

Last day? It seems unlikely, for already plans are underway for the third test — Charlie Test, in Navy lingo — which is to be the firing of a bomb deep in water. The other day I was back at the southwestern end of the atoll, at the pretty island of Oruk, and there I saw the first preparations for Charlie Test. The engineers had anchored an enormous cable into the solid coral of the island. From there the chain stretched out across the shallows and plunged over the barrier reef into deep water. The plan is to stretch that cable out and anchor the far end a mile or so offshore. From this giant common mooring numerous smaller chains may be brought to the surface at spaced intervals upon which the ships of that deep-water test may be securely fastened. Test Charlie therefore is becoming a reality, and most of us expect to be here six months from now when the test is scheduled.

But for now the task force is moving to the better winter anchorage of Kwajalein Atoll. Most of the ships have gone. Those of the target fleet not worth saving will be sunk by gunfire; the rest of the grim, disfigured fleet are getting underway, obediently drifting behind their tugs: the carrier *Independence*, her flight deck plowed up by the first Bomb; the attack transport *Fallon*, with a mighty list to starboard; the destroyer *Hughes*, lifeless and mottled a dirty brown from numberless futile washings. One by one they are stringing out through Enyu Channel on the long tow to Kwaj.

The *Haven* got underway late in the afternoon. As we slipped out over the green opalescence of the bar a tremendous explosion took place on the shore of Bikini Island, where the Seabees are blasting some sort of channel in the barrier reef. It must have been a real charge, a sort of farewell salute, for the white cloud boiled up from behind the palms, ascending rapidly to several thousand feet and then mushrooming out into a magnificent plume. It looked like a miniature atomic explosion, and served to make us reflect on why we had come all the way to Bikini to do a job which no one wanted done, which everyone was afraid of. It made us wonder what we had learned, what use all the carloads of reports and graphs would be, were we ever faced with these problems again outside of the fascinating laboratory of Bikini.

The little island, canopied in palms, and the ruddy sun dropped away together into the sea. Bikini, which once was inhabited by a hundred Marshallese, which once belonged to the Germans, and then to the Japanese, now belongs to an unknown future along with Hiroshima and Nagasaki.

Friday, August 30

Kwajalein Atoll. Most of our Bikini fleet is here, anchored well out in the main harbor. We have not been the most welcome of visitors. In fact, we are not yet allowed ashore at all except on special missions. Anyone who has been connected with Operation Crossroads is a leper here.

Rain today, all day. Not the usual cloudburst of sunshine but cold gray monotonous drizzle. October rain, with the gaunt ships looking as drab and dispirited as the leafless elms in an October drizzle. A pattern of gray outside, and of melancholy within.

Monday, September 2

Once again the laboratory is to dedicate itself to the mysteries of urinalysis for radioactivity. There are no new dangers out here. The ships, if anything, are safer today than a month ago, and most of the work aboard them is limited to pumping them out and emptying the magazines of ammunition which might in time become dangerous. But the problem of day-to-day exposure continues and so the check must continue.

Fortunately the number to be studied is much less than before, and thanks to a technique worked out by Carter and Huff, we can now do urinalysis much more accurately than before. Because a slight rise above background in counts per minute may indicate the presence of dangerous amounts of radioactive materials in the body of the person in question, the most meticulous analysis is none too good. Ideally one should have (1) a twenty-four hour sample taken immediately following exposure, and under conditions of absolute cleanliness, (2) clean, unused pipettes, dishes and so on, (3) counters with low backgrounds (uncontaminated) so that small changes may be greater than the normal variations of the instrument, and (4) long counts so as to minimize the factor of variation in the counter.

None of these conditions can be met out here. Unfortunately there is just no way to simplify this problem. By the method of Carter and Huff we take ten cubic centimeters of urine, and evaporate it to dryness in a little dish which has previously been checked for radioactivity on a sensitive counter. The dried film of urine is then counted for three minutes on the cleanest beta-gamma counters we have. If any show a significant increase in counts, the pan is recounted, and 100 cc. of the urine boiled down, ashed with boiling nitric and sulphuric acids, and the ash recounted for five or ten minutes.

It sounds scientific. Actually it is a most crude screening device. The biological effects of radiation impose the most stringent conditions, and those who are inclined to rejoice in the coming of atomic energy for peaceful purposes, along with those who minimize the dangers of atomic warfare, should at least understand these conditions. This philosophical question, however, has no place out here. We can at best only do sixty to a hundred samples in a day. The lab and the corridors reek of the fumes of our work, and we are subjected to the continuing abuse of our fellow men whose lives and futures we are supposed to be interested in protecting.

Wednesday, September 4

Kwaj is a dismal island, not an outpost of the Navy, not a crossroads of the Pacific, but a back alley, a junk pile. Its lagoon shore is littered with the debris of military campaigns and military occupation, half buried in sand and rust. Its oceanward vista is even more desolate. The muddy roads lead down between rows of barracks and storehouses, most of them locked and showing signs of the rapid dilapidation of the tropics. The airstrip still does a fair amount of business, being the main stopping point between Pearl and Guam; and the two officers' clubs have an air of relaxed and amiable somnolence.

Peace has come, and man's slow pace can never keep up to the molds, the weeds, the rust.

Across the great landing strip, on the southeast side of the island, almost on the ocean, is a group of five Quonset huts which not so long ago were the technical center for Operation Crossroads. Here in lead and cement encased vaults were kept the mysterious components of those two Bombs. Here the experts worked, assembling the masses of fissionable material in barely subcritical amounts. With faith in their slide rules, in their micrograms and millimeters, they set up the delicate detonating mechanisms for Able and Baker Days.

The buildings remain, empty now, except for two which were used as laboratories. It was to these laboratories that we made several pilgrimages in hopes of finding chemicals and electronic equipment for our primitive laboratories on the *Haven*. Out of the chaos of smashed and discarded glassware, counters, balances, Bunsen burners, and so forth, we were able to salvage quite a lot of useful gear. One of the interesting items was a blackboard on which was scribbled a series of chemical symbols and a lot of calculations. Some of it was recognizable, but most of it offered little for the most fertile imaginations.

Like the ubiquitous Kilroy, the atomic scientists had scribbled in effect, "The Manhattan District was here," and had departed. How like America, even, it seems.

Here, as there, enshrouded in darkness and barbed wire, the unknown scientists had come to work on their unmentionable discoveries, communicated in their strange language and hieroglyphics, set up and conducted their experiments, and then vanished, leaving only a scribbled note, "The Manhattan District was here."

How like America, where only the very few know what is really going on behind the darkness and barbed wire, or what effect it will have upon the living and the unborn.

Sunday, September 8

We are still riding our anchor chains here in Kwajalein and see little sign of change. The fleet of dead ships is still afloat, and little by little the ammunition is being carried off the larger vessels. They stand near by, crippled, gaunt, silent, the twisted wreckage, still untouched on deck, creaking with the slow rolling of the ships. They box the compass with the variable winds, and disappear for a while in the rain squalls. But back again they emerge, and we wonder what in hell to do with them.

It used to be that we could escape from it all for a few hours by going up to the nav deck and watching the evening movie picture. Since the departure of the main fleet the pictures have been so uniformly unbearable that only those already psychotic could sit through them.

Thursday, September 12

Kwajalein Harbor is full of strange ships, eyed with suspicion by the shore-based Navy, and with despair by the Crossroads Navy. Among the quarantined fleet is a particularly interesting ship. It is a great greasy black tub, with a bluff bow, low sides, and a dormitory-like structure extending nearly the full length of its wide deck. It is, or was, a sort of floating barracks, having large rooms, mess halls, showers, locker rooms, etc. When it became evident that boarding parties were tracking back quantities of radioactivity into their clean vessels, and thus endangering the whole Radiological Safety program, this seagoing shore installation was transformed into a sort of locker and shower and clothing-issue room for all parties going to the target ships.

Today I had the duty with an ammunition unloading party aboard the *Independence*. One enters the change ship from one side, and in some distant locker room is given an issue of freshly laundered fatigues, along with boots, rubber gloves, and oxygen rebreathing gear. Thus equipped, the party is assembled and transported to its destination. Once alongside you strap on your oxygen gear and face mask, and stumble over the side and climb the boarding nets.

The *Independence* is a ghost ship — its flight deck blown up, leaving the thick oak planks broken like so much boxwood; its hangar deck blasted down and only the skeleton of the sides remaining. Gun turrets and gangways, twisted, crushed, dangle oversides, grating and creaking with the roll of the ship. Doors are smashed in and jammed tight against the bulkheads, or blown out altogether, and the rusty water sloshes aimlessly back and forth across the rusty decks. For the most part the radiation is not particularly high, although sometimes these rusty pools will set your earphones singing and shoot your indicator needles off scale.

The route to the magazines is a maze of gangways and black passages barely visible through the bleary oxygen masks and the constant streams of sweat which fill one's eyes. Each passageway and each new compartment has to be inspected for poisonous gases and for radiation. It was not our mission to remove any ammunition, merely to open up the passages and okay them for later parties. Many of the ships were heavily loaded with ammo, from machine-gun rounds on up to torpedoes. The process of unloading seems at the moment a truly Herculean assignment. A man can work only about thirty minutes in an oxygen rebreather; then he must go on deck and get some air, a cigarette, and a chance to release the steam from beneath his collar. Two hours aboard, under such conditions, is a day's work.

After that, back to the floating barracks. Here the boots are scrubbed with soapy water, and the clothing discarded to be laundered or buried at sea, depending upon the degree of contamination. The cost of even such minimal activities as we now engage in, in terms of clothing, boots, gloves, and oxygen rebreathing gear, and in terms of the gigantic daily laundry operations, must be staggering.

To the sailors it must all be incomprehensible. Here we are insisting on measures of extreme caution at a time when the radiation has had a month and a half to decay away, when the ships' decks are probably not a thousandth as hot as they were in the first hour following the Baker explosion. These same measures were not employed in the first weeks, why then now?

There are good reasons. In the first place, it is a good policy in public or industrial health to be as cautious and conservative as is consistent with the job to be done. In the first hectic week or two following the last shot when ships had to be pumped or left to sink, when there were important instruments and experimental animals to recover, and when the problem of decontamination was less well understood – in those days, if such extreme precautions had been required, nothing at all could have been done and the experiment would have been a total failure. We were in a position similar (though infinitely better probably) to that of a city bombed out with atomic weapons. No such rigmarole as rubber boots and gloves and oxygen rebreathing masks could conceivably be used if San Francisco were atomized, its population struggling to escape from the blazing debris, the smoke, and the terror of the unseen emanations.

But out here we are under no such duress. The experiment is largely done. Our job is merely janitorial, and so maximum precautions consistent with our simple tasks are justified.

There is another good reason; the very fact that radioactivity is apparently decaying away makes caution the more imperative. This paradoxical statement is based upon the presence of dangerous materials which are not detectable on the ordinary Geiger counter, notably remnants of the plutonium of the original Bomb. As the telltale radiation decays away our sense of security therefrom may be entirely false.

This theoretical situation has been pretty well borne out by the experimental work of Lars and Tom in the laboratory. Lars has made an intensive study of the rate of radioactive decay of many samples of material — paint, rust, wood, glass, rope, brass, calking, coral, algae, and so forth. His graphs show a steady, predictable trend covering a month. The rate of that process is now becoming very slow. We have lost those components from the original blast which had short half lives, a matter of seconds, hours, or days. Those that remain now, a month and a half later, have half lives which will extend for years or centuries, or even longer. Therefore, we can expect little change in the intensity, except through day-to-day weathering and rusting.

Simultaneous with Lars's work has been that of Tom, who has become our specialist in alpha detection. The use of that precious alpha counter — of which we have only one, securely hidden away in an isolated part of the laboratory — requires considerable training and experience, and Tom, after weeks of painstaking work, has become a reliable operator. His results consistently show that there is a small but definite amount of plutonium spread atom-thin over most of the contaminated areas. Comparing the work of these two studies, one cannot escape the conclusion that the relative danger from plutonium must necessarily increase in proportion as the shorter-lived beta-gamma emitters (our warning signals) appear to be dying away.

Monday, September 16

The weather is steadily growing worse, with ever fewer sunny recesses between rain squalls. The laboratory is still preoccupied with boiling urine, and the rest of the task force with its ammunition disposal. Neither job has many enthusiasts, and neither seems to have any ending.

In the past weeks our target ships have become a dismal sight, rusty, unkempt, useless. Even the beautiful *Prinz Eugen*, once the pride of the German Fleet and as sleek and cavalier a ship as ever sailed the seas, looks as drab as the sorriest tin can. Uninjured physically by either of the blasts, she is nevertheless dying of a malignant disease for which there is no help.

Efforts at decontamination have come to a standstill

with total defeat for the magic powers of soap and water. As a matter of fact, Tom, Lars, and Rex Huff have demonstrated in the laboratory that fission products can be removed only by taking off the outer surface of the area in question. They have been able, by means of strong acid, to remove most radioactivity from samples of paint, steel, and so on. It works in a test tube, but a test tube is not where most of us live. The problem of decontaminating the total surface of a battleship or the brick and cement of a future Hiroshima remains practically insoluble.

The same applies to much of our laboratory work. How can we translate our findings into the severely practical necessities of everyday life? Einstein's famous formula equating mass and energy seems harmless enough on paper. Meitner and Hahn, who discovered fission, and Fermi, who proved that a chain reaction was possible, seemed to be minding their own business, the search for scientific truth. But their work, taken from its laboratory context, has become a judgment against life itself.

Not many of the studies we have been interested in have an application only to pure science. For example, we have been trying to discover whether or not the degree of radioactivity present in Bikini water after the Baker test has harmed the metabolic processes of marine life. We can compare, in a crude way, the capacity of algae, exposed and unexposed, to produce oxygen in the presence of light as a by-product to photosynthesis. We can make radio-autographs of the distribution of radio-activity in the bodies of little fish, and by means of fish population surveys attempt to discover whether or not the Bomb had any effect on the life cycles of the lagoon inhabitants. Such studies are important. They should indeed be carried on by men more competent in these fields than any of us, and above all they should be continued for months or even years, if necessary, so that the true picture may be known.

This is not merely academic. Such studies may influence the lives of people living in the Tibetan plateau. We don't know to what distances from Bikini the radiation disease may be carried. We can't predict to what degree the balance of nature will be thrown off by atomic bombs. We certainly have little idea what the long-range effects on our lives would be from an all-out atomic war, devastating our shores, our fish, and our agricultural industries. But at least at this time we do know that Bikini is not some faraway little atoll pinpointed on an out-of-the-way chart. Bikini is San Francisco Bay, Puget Sound, East River. It is the Thames, the Adriatic, Hellespont, and misty Baikal. It isn't just King Juda and his displaced native subjects about whom we have to think — or to forget.

There is so much to do, and so little time and experience with which to do it.

I was standing by the rail watching an oncoming squall and thinking of the routines with which the laboratory was preoccupied when Commander Harris came alongside.

"I've got good news for you, Bradley."

I had heard that approach before, heralding some calamity.

"Good news, Commander Harris? You mean that some battlewagon is coming in with three thousand more urine specimens to run?"

He chuckled and shook his head. "No, not this time. You remember the fishing trip we talked about. Well, I put in a request for it weeks ago, and today I got the okay from the Admiral."

That was indeed wonderful news. Long ago, hearing that some ill-advised sailors had been eating fish caught in the vicinity of Bikini, we recommended early and repeated surveys of the atolls surrounding Bikini: Eniwetok to the west, and a number of little atolls to the east. But at that time there was too much going on to be bothered with such research, and so the idea had been shelved.

"You will have a mine sweeper, under the command of Captain Clancy," Commander Harris went on. "Clancy has become quite a well-known fisherman out here. He's taken a lot of the big guns out, Admiral Blandy among them, and he really knows his stuff."

"How far will we go, Eniwetok?"

"No. The Admiral felt that that wasn't necessary. No, to Wotho, Rongerik, and Rongelap. If you find anything there perhaps we can talk the Admiral into a further trip later on. You'd better go over to see Clancy and make arrangements with him."

"Yes, sir, and thanks a lot."

Commander Harris rubbed his sunburned head reflectively, and sighed: "Should be a wonderful trip. I wish I could go myself."

As soon as a motorboat was available I took off for YMS 358 (Yard Mine Sweeper). I found George Clancy engaged in supervising the aquatics of his crew. A slight, blond, bright-eyed young man, nothing like the leathery old salt I had expected, he was dressed in swimming trunks and a baseball cap. Stationed on the after rail of his tiny mine sweeper, he fondled a carbine and kept a sharp lookout for sharks. Clancy had heard of the proposed fishing trip, and although he had been doing practically nothing but fishing steadily for the past four months, he was enthusiastic about setting forth again.

"Only let's wait till I get my stove fixed up, Doc," he said. "The last trip out we ate nothing but cold Spam for three weeks. If I ever have to eat Spam again, it's gonna be with the can still on."

It was easy to make plans with Clancy, and just as I was ready to go he asked: "By the way, Doc, you're one of these Geiger pilots. Do you think it is safe for my men to be swimming around the ship?"

"How do you mean? From sharks?" I asked.

"Oh, no. We can take care of them okay," he laughed,

indicating his carbine. "No, but from the Geigers. We've been laying around a lot in Bikini and our bottom's pretty fouled up. A Geiger man came over the other day and found stuff all through our water coolers. Some of the boys are married and are pretty worried."

Clancy was well briefed on radiation, and wanted to know whether there was any danger to the men sleeping next to the hull from radiation coming through from the outside. Fortunately, I had a Geiger counter with me, and suggested having one of the swimmers pick up some grass from the bottom of the boat. That, however, Clancy would not do, and handing the gun to his chief engineer he dove over himself to collect the algae. It showed little activity, no more than any of the Bikini fleet. We had found the same low activity on the *Haven*'s algae after making the trip down from Bikini to Kwaj. Either the fission products had been washed off, or they had been replaced by non-radioactive isotopes present in the pure sea water. We were inclined to favor the latter process since washing above decks had proved so ineffectual.

After that we made a survey of the entire ship, finding some contamination in the coolers, and in the salt-water mains, but nothing hazardous unless the coolers were to be overhauled and scaled out. The skipper and crew, thus reassured, were ready to begin their fishing trip, as soon as the stove was repaired, a matter of but a few days. I was glad to be able to look over their ship and to answer their questions. There must be thousands of Navy men exactly like Clancy and his crew, who did their job at Bikini because it was their assignment and who will live henceforth in a sort of vague and needless anxiety about those mysterious "Geigers." Radiation sickness is a definite and predictable disease. We know more about it than we do of measles; its characteristics should become common knowledge. They are real and impressive enough without investing them in the terrors of the supernatural.

Sunday, September 29

The interlude aboard YMS 358 is done. The fishing trip a complete success. We now understand for the first time why so many people want to be President. Even now I couldn't chronicle that trip in separate days; the days and nights of that delightful cruise passed as one continuous manic state, and the changing scene, regardless of how varied, seemed to be all part of a single magnificent scheme, much as a dream seems to the dreamer.

Five of us there were: Lars, Tom, Carter, and I from the Radiological Safety Section, and Chief Engineer Chris Christiansen. Six days ago, of this group, only Chris knew anything about tuna fishing. Captain Clancy and his crew, of course, were experts. We came aboard with our gear in the midafternoon, and almost before we had the tackle over the side Clancy had his mine sweeper underway. Out through the oilers, the gasoline ships, the cement-sided floating dry docks we steamed, then out through the dead fleet, looking as forgotten as stone implements in a museum case, and finally, just at sundown, out through Gea Pass into the open ocean.

Our ship turned out to be wonderfully suited to our needs, being of shallow draught, maneuverable, and not too fast. She was perhaps a hundred feet overall. The ship's complement was three officers and twenty-five men. There were no extra bunks, and so we quartered on cots out on the forecastle deck, where the steamy singing of the engines and the rush of wind and waves made sleep something so wonderful you'd like to stay awake for it, a rare experience aboard ship in the tropics. We took our meals — when there was time for meals — with the skipper, and although the wardroom was so minute we must eat in shifts, Captain Clancy's expansive personality made each mealtime a banquet.

Clancy, a young Annapolis graduate, was one of those euphoric Irishmen, independent, capable, and having shamrock juice running in their veins, who are born skippers of ships and leaders of men. In all our days aboard he rarely wore anything more than skivvies and a baseball cap. He seemed to know everything that was going on aboard his ship at all times. Barefooted, he clambered around from galley to bridge to engine room, obviously enamored of every plank and plate of the gray old vessel that was "his." A tireless fisherman, by day he directed our amateurish activities on the fantail, or sat astride of the rail on the bridge, guiding the ship into the luminous turquoise waters, just outside of the barrier reefs where the fishing is best. At night in the tiny wardroom he was an equally tireless and exuberant raconteur, a delightful hedonist. I don't think he ever slept. When it came time to sack out, Clancy invariably went aloft to the bridge to keep an eye on things while his ship sniffed her way through the coral-patterned sea.

His crew of twenty-five men, mostly youngsters, admired him and seemed imbued with the same infectious zest for life that he had. To them he was a big brother, coach, chaplain, and Admiral Halsey all rolled into one, and though he was only twenty-two he was affectionately referred to as "the old man."

On successive days we touched at Wotho, Rongerik, Rongelap, and Aelinginai atolls, finding the fishing better than we had expected.

What did we accomplish — from a scientific point of view, that is? We caught over sixty seagoing fish — tunas, jacks, wahoos, and others — and in none was there any evidence of radioactivity, either by rough examination of their opened viscera, or later by careful beta-counting of slices of their preserved livers. And for all good Waltonians I should add that the fish were so large we lost half as many more, including several sharks, on broken tackle.

One cannot conclude from our findings that fish bearing radioactive material are not radiating out from the tiny source at Bikini, from one atoll to another, perhaps to great distances, or that they won't at a later time thus disseminate the contamination of that second shot. Studies of this sort should be repeated at ever widening intervals of time and space so that we will know to what degree an atomic explosion in one locality may menace some far-distant population of marine or human life.

On the first day out, we completely circumnavigated the little atoll of Wotho and we had excellent fishing. For nearly the entire circuit we were escorted by a school of porpoises who breached and barrel-rolled between us and the jagged barrier as though standing guard lest we get too close.

On the second morning there was Rongerik coming up with the dawn just as Captain Clancy and the radar had said. Fishing at Rongerik was known to be poor, and we found it so. There was only one flurry of excitement, when we ran across a school of wahoos. In an instant all five of our lines leaped into life, and an instant later three had snapped. The two wahoos we managed to land were our biggest fish, the largest weighing 42 pounds. It took three men to land him.

We fished only the east shore line, and at one point, where the barrier lay just offshore from a densely verdured islet, two natives appeared on the sandy bank, barefoot and wearing the usual castoff Navy dungarees. They watched us pass, making solemn gestures for us to come ashore. These were natives of Bikini, transplanted to Rongerik some six months ago. They were known to be none too happy in their foster atoll.

That afternoon we entered the quiet lagoon through the usual southeast passage, which so many atolls seem to have, and steering between the easily visible coral heads Captain Clancy found a berth for his ship not far from the main island of Rongerik. It was one of those bright but ominous afternoons, with the wind down and the giant thunderheads standing all around as though waiting for some signal to move in. The glassy surface of the lagoon mirrored the limp sail of a native canoe returning from one of the other islands. As we neared the main island several small outriggers put out to convoy us in, their occupants sitting crosslegged on the thwart, alternately paddling and bailing their roughhewn canoes. They greeted us with wide, toothless smiles, and before our anchor rattled to the bottom they had made fast astern and clambered over the side.

The Bikinese are mild, friendly people; in no way like the giant cannibals of the Fijis, they are short, their hair is long and wavy, and their skin is a soft dark brown. They greeted everyone aboard, from the skipper to the most youthful, with a dignified and sonorous "Good — day — how are you," supplemented by a solemn and completely limp handshake.

Only one could speak any English. He announced himself with:

"My name is Pillip. I come Kwaj'lin Atoll. I come to teach English here very much."

He spoke some English, and if given time seemed to understand it. Pillip's office and his person were dignified by a white shirt and a pair of castoff GI galoshes which were at least six sizes too large for him. He was obviously very proud of his robes of state. Evidently he had been deputized by King Juda to make a plea to the skipper, and he lost no time in approaching Clancy.

"My name is Pillip. Now I shall tell you something of myself. We . . . We [with a gesture indicating his companions] are very hungry. We . . . have nothing to eat . . . yes. Now I shall tell you something about this island. This is . . . a very poor island. We . . . have not enough coconuts . . . no. For many days now we eat nothing but fish."

Clancy knew his business. He listened respectfully to the sermon and then began to feel his way along the channel which leads to a good bargain with the natives. He did not drive a hard bargain, but a fair one, mostly for the fun of the game, and the natives were delighted to learn that in time they might have some flour, sugar, cigarettes, and fishhooks. The Captain then, with great ceremony, was invited ashore, and the boat lowered away for him. As for the promised flour and sugar, the natives did not trust our skiff, preferring to take their precious cargo ashore in their little one-man outrigger canoes.

Most of the villagers were clustered on the beach. Lusty hands pulled the boat high on the sand almost before we could jump out. There was a lot more of the ceremonious handshaking, and then we were introduced to the chief, King Juda. He was a leathery old fellow, with silver hair, whose regal vestments consisted of a somewhat tattered white shirt. He spoke no English, but gave us a cordial welcome and invited us to be his guests at the palace in the village. Thither we went, King Juda leading the way, and followed by a comet's tail of little children. After them came the men, respectful and solemn; the women had not come to the beach. They stood with their babes in arms silently under the trees.

The reception room was a large open-air porch adjoining the king's house. A rickety table and a still more rickety bench were placed at one end for us. We all sat down, and since Pillip, the only one who spoke English, was still on the beach bringing in the loot, nothing was said for a long time. Meanwhile most of the men of the village collected inside the room, squatting on their haunches on the sand. The women shuffled about the periphery with the vague curiosity and reflective air of chickens scratching around in a barnyard. After minutes of this petrified pantomime I got restless, but seeing Clancy calmly and confidently waiting, imperturbably balanced on that antique bench, I realized that there must be some obscure plan in all this and that they also will be served who only sit and wait.

Sure enough, eventually the wife of Pillip came shuffling across the village in that slow, flat-footed method of locomotion characteristic of these women. She was formally introduced, and explained that the king was glad to welcome us, that Rongerik was a very poor island, that there were not sufficient palms to support a population of 160 people.

"Every day we eat fish. Nothing but fish. Someday I think we all become like birds."

There was no humor attached to this flight of imagination. Captain Clancy then replied that he had ordered flour, sugar, coffee, cigarettes, and other items to be brought ashore. When this was translated there was a great show of approval among the seated watchers. The king rose to deliver an oration of thanksgiving, and after another round of handshaking, invited us to see his village, asking the lady to serve as our guide.

The little settlement was, of course, very small, consisting of perhaps a score of buildings clustered under the largest palms near the shore. Most of the homes were made of wooden frames whose timbers were lashed together with twine, over which a thick covering of pandanus and thatching had been carefully worked. They were airy, but comfortable and very clean. The floors were made either of white coral sand or of sheets of plywood left by the Seabees who had brought them here from Bikini. Some of the houses had colorful patterns and decorations woven into the walls and window borders.

At intervals throughout the village the Seabees had erected sloping rain traps of corrugated sheet roofing which drained into cisterns and constituted thereby the only source of water for these people. In the neighboring island of Rongelap, which we visited on another day, water was gathered from the palms much as a New Englander gathers his maple sap in the late winter.

Life drifts along more or less becalmed in these native villages. There are no pressing duties to be done. The men paddle off to their fishing grounds when they feel like it, and when they return the catch is distributed and often eaten right on the beach without so much as cooking or cleaning the fish. The older men sit cross-legged on the sand, chipping away on logs with a kind of adz, out of which eventually they fashion their canoes. The children move around in little animated groups, surging back and forth like schools of minnows. When hungry, they tear their fish apart with fingers and teeth, or break open a coconut and gnaw the white meat out of the fragments.

But youth and energy are soon lost. Girls before they bear their first children begin to sag and slouch and shuffle along, and in the course of a few seasons of fertility pass into that deliberate, soggy, breast-weary somnambulation which characterizes their appearance for the latter half of their lives.

The sun had come and gone, and the promised rain came in sheets and gray gusts across the lagoon. The once limp and becalmed fishing boat filled its woven sail, kicked up its outrigger and came scudding into the beach, where it was hauled up among the trees with the other boats.

And then sun again! Back at the reception hall I found Clancy and a few of the others still seated on that booby trap of a bench. King Juda was there too, looking placidly on. Nothing seemed to be happening, but the skipper apparently knew what he was doing. Eventually the table began to bear the fruit of patience as one after another of the people shuffled up with gifts: shells, some of them exquisitely patterned by nature, and many hand-made objects of art in the form of woven bags, fans, belts wrought with small shells, grass skirts. Such things seem to have no part in native life, but are known to be the souvenirs sought by white sailors. They were offered to the Captain in gratitude for the food and as a symbol of hospitality.

When the gifts had all been presented, Clancy thanked the king for his friendliness and the generosity of his people. Then the king rose and delivered himself of another oration, at the end of which Pillip explained that King Juda would like to know when he and his people might be able to return to Bikini. This was a question for which King Juda and his imperturbable people had more than the ordinary concern, and it was no pleasant task to have to inform him that we thought it would be a long time yet. We tried to explain how the trees and the village had been pretty well destroyed and how the water and the fish were still unsafe and might be for months and years to come. Of such things, these people could understand nothing, but their feelings were unmistakable. Pillip delivered his shortest and most impassioned oration of the day when he said sadly and respectfully, "Oh. We very sorry to hear this."

The Bikinese, 160 odd people, are not the first, nor will they be the last, to be left homeless and impoverished by the inexorable Bomb. They have no choice in the matter, and very little understanding of it. But in this perhaps they are not so different from us all.

The trip passed by rapidly, the days and nights merging into a continuous stream of happy events. None of us were great fishermen, but who could fail to be tugged from his lethargy by a hand-to-hand battle with a thirty-pound yellow-fin tuna? There was something almost dreamlike about coasting along beside the foaming barrier reefs, looking out over the surf to the placid turquoise lagoons and their brilliant sand bars and humid little islets.

Monday, September 30

Kwaj has not changed during our week away; it occupies the same vacuum in space and time it did a week ago. Nothing has changed; nothing is new save the fact that the rear guard of Joint Task Force One is moving ashore in order to release ships like the *Haven* for more active duty. We shall take up quarters in the five Quonset huts on the far side of the island originally occupied by the two Bombs and their attendants.

It would seem that our work out here is about at an end. The derelict fleet may go on indefinitely, being pumped out as indicated, or towed away to sink. The radioactivity over the ships' decks and superstructures has settled down to the substances whose half lives may be hundreds and thousands of years — eternity for all practical purposes. All thought of decontaminating them and getting them underway again is, of course, out of the question, and except for the effects of weathering and rusting, one could study these ships as well ten years from now as today. The recent announcement by the President, canceling Charlie Test (the deep-water shot), would seem to be the final *coup de grâce* for Operation Crossroads.

The Crossroads tests at first glance might seem to have been a failure. From a military point of view the two shots confirmed what was already known of the effectiveness of a chain reaction as an explosive, and certainly proved, beyond all expectations, what was feared concerning the poisoning of land, sea, and air with radioactivity. Scientifically what was learned in the crude laboratory of Bikini remains to be evaluated and declassified from the archives of military secrecy.

But the greatest failure of all in these tests has been in apprehending their sociological implications. Evidently the Bomb has failed to impress more than a few congenital pessimists with the full scope of its lethal potential. This error in publicity — an error of omission — might be justifiable on the basis of strict military secrecy. In the long run, however, the one thing more dangerous than informed governments abroad will be an uninformed American opinion.

The question is not political so much as biological. It is not the security of a political system but the survival of the race that is at stake in the indiscriminate use of atomic energy for political coercion. Its unique problems are self-evident; there is nothing about them so profound as to require translation by a scientist. Among them are:

(1) There is no real defense against atomic weapons.

(2) There are no satisfactory countermeasures and methods of decontamination.

(3) There are no satisfactory medical or sanitary safeguards for the people of atomized areas.

(4) The devastating influence of the Bomb and its unborn relatives may affect the land and its wealth — and therefore its people — for centuries through the persistence of radioactivity.

These facts are substantiated in theory by experiments upon thousands of animals, and in practice by Hiroshima, Nagasaki, and Bikini. It is in this sense that the Crossroads tests have been anything but failures. Hastily planned and hastily carried out, they may have only sketched in the gross outlines of the real problem; nevertheless, those outlines show pretty clearly the shadow of the colossus which looms behind tomorrow.

Wednesday and Thursday, October 9 and 10

With the abruptness and finality of orders in the Army we received our transfer back to the United States duty and separation from Crossroads. Late in the afternoon a NATS DC–4 came in from Guam with space available for Tom, Lars, and me. We were packed and ready at the airport within a half hour. As the great silvery ship, humming with power, lifted itself from the runway, passed over the Marine barracks, the huts, the post office, and up over the line of curling surf, we had our last glimpse of the spectral fleet. There lay the *Nevada*, still a proud cardinal with its tail feathers burned off; there were the *Pensacola* and *Salt Lake City*, their superstructures dangling crazily oversides; there too the sturdy sullen *New York*, the destroyers streaked with foamite and rust, the *Prinz Eugen*, still the most beautiful ship of its kind afloat, and far in the distance the *Independence*, an exploded myth of military security.

Looking down at the lagoon with its toy flotilla, I wondered if we were really succeeding in running away. Radioactivity, contamination, the wrecked island of Bikini and its sad-eyed patient exiles — could they ever be eluded? Maybe not, but at least somebody else was taking over the graveyard shift, and for the moment we were happy in the illusion of escape. Like one waking from the toils of a nightmare we welcomed the black night and the thousands of miles of black Pacific beneath. Johnston Island came and went, a pin point of light in all that empty ocean, an island no bigger for us than the glare of the landing lights on the field, and the snack bar, with its bustle of sleepy-eyed patrons. Then Hawaii, like a beautiful monarch moth, half emerging from a cocoon of mist.

That evening we took off again and spent a long night in the comfortless darkness of bucket seats. Fourteen hours later the rugged coastline and golden hills of California were just shaking off the blanket of fog when we first saw them. How beautiful! How peaceful and prosperous! How wonderful to be home again! We wanted so much to return to the America we had left — a country victorious and magnanimous in war, a country still confident in its ways of peace. Minutes later we were down to the ground.

Everything looked the same. The people were busy and happy, well fed and well amused. There was the glittering city of San Francisco, in its customary euphoria. The tides of business and pleasure across its fabulous bridges were running at a flood. At night the whole bay area seemed like a bright nebula in the milky way of American prosperity.

We were surprised at first to find so little interest in the Bikini tests. But we really had no right to be. Atomic energy was an uncomfortable subject. Things like John

Hersey's *Hiroshima* were rough. How much more pleasant to consider the coming miracles of healing, the prolongation of life, the days of sunny leisure which people were everywhere promising. People were having troubles enough anyway. Why let in the bogeyman to the sweet dreams of atomic energy for peacetime purposes?

August 6, 1945. The first experimental city, Hiroshima.

1945. Nagasaki. "They make a desert and call it peace." — Tacitus.

1946. Exiles. Three Bikinians on Rongerik.

1953. Nevada. Testing a 200 millimeter nuclear shell. The U.S. and U.S.S.R. have approximately 30,000 of these "tactical weapons."

1956. Bikini Atoll. A large hydrogen bomb eruption as seen from 50 miles. The area of total destruction might be up to 10 miles in radius, with serious burns as far away as 20 or 30 miles.

EPILOGUE

Thither we sailed, and some god
guided us through the night,
for it was dark, a mist lying
deep about the ships. . . .

—ODYSSEUS

I

WHEN THE MESSAGE sped from Chicago to Washington, in December 1942, *The Italian navigator has safely landed in the New World,* reporting in code that Enrico Fermi's chain reaction had worked, it is doubtful that any of the scientists realized the irony of their words. "Safely" meant only that the pile of carbon bricks and purified uranium under Stagg Stadium hadn't blown itself up. And as for the "New World," nothing beyond an immediate shoreline was visible.

Yet very soon farsighted men began to see the contours of that world, among them Bohr the Dane, Szilard the Hungarian, Einstein the German. It was a world of power and danger unlike anything human beings had known before. Niels Bohr was the first of the seers,

Copenhagen's famous nuclear physicist, a big, funny, courageous fellow, a St. Bernard of a man. In the American–British policy of excluding our ally Russia from any knowledge of the atom bomb work, Bohr foresaw the coming cold war. He knew too well the Russian physicists and the traditions of science in that country not to believe they would soon learn of the Manhattan Project and begin building their own atom bomb works. Then would pile up a cumulus of resentment and suspicion that would grow into an arms storm.

Bohr spent two years of the war trying to persuade Roosevelt and Churchill to give up their faith in secrecy and monopoly. But Roosevelt knew little of Russians and still less of physics; he treated the good Dane to a sight-seeing tour of wartime Washington offices. Churchill wanted Bohr locked up.

Thus the New World lost its first statesman and its first and best chance to take control of that portentous chain reaction.

But in 1945 there seemed to be so much time. We looked upon our secret power with wondrous, sunny insouciance. General Groves assured us the Russians would not crack the secret for 50 years. We wanted to believe him, we did believe him; the Russians proved him wrong by 46 years.

As for the 1946 tests at Bikini atoll, they were a dandy Fourth of July celebration intended to demonstrate America's supreme science and scare the troublemakers abroad. Who cared if it ruined some old ships? We had the bomb and the bomb would take care of the future.

If our blowing up more atom bombs in the far Pacific made people uneasy, they could thank the French for a happy diversion. The French conducted tests of their own. They took one of their St. Tropez mammoexotics, called her the Anatomic Bomb, decked her out in threads, and created "the bikini." The clever French humanized the chain reaction, made a seashore spectacle of it and a marketing triumph as well. The old world was getting its nerve back.

Still there were uneasy premonitions. A few months after the tests at Bikini, the editor of the *Chicago Tribune* called Leo Szilard at the University of Chicago: "If one of those bombs goes off in Lake Michigan all that hot stuff could come down all over Chicago — right?"

"Right."

"Well, what about the water? We use a lot of water at this plant. Is there any way to filter out those geigers?"

Szilard, one of the original bomb physicists and a pixilated one, assured the editor that any good industrial filter would take out most of the "geigers." Then he said, "But let me ask you, sir. . . . If those bombs go off in Lake Michigan, to whom will you sell your papers?"

Like the *Chicago Tribune* editor, most of us come to Einstein's universe with only ten fingers to count with.

We can read of the ships at Bikini, but we can't imagine Chicago empty, abandoned for 200 years. We can read of Hiroshima, but we don't see the City of Brotherly Love in ashes or Washington, that great city, another Babylon.

Instinct has preserved us so far. After the two bombs that ended World War II, human beings, in spite of many provocations, have carefully avoided using atomic weapons. Instinct — a kind of certainty surer than knowledge — will have to guide us in the future. Instinct and the courage to keep on.

Not much in history or mathematics prepares us to deal with the atomic world. In the days of Troy, war was already a destroyer of cities, total and unconditional: babies to the sword, women to the wheel, civilization to the torch. We have it on good authority that in those times it took all the best fighting men from all the kingdoms of Greece ten years (and some slick trickery) to pull down one small walled city.

Three thousand years later, in the Second World War, things were not very different. The Allies sometimes sent a thousand planes a day over Germany, carrying tens of thousands of tons of explosives and hundreds of thousands of phosphorous firebombs. Yet it took five years to bring the German cities to surrender.

And then in 1945 on a fair, breezy, sunny summer morning at exactly 8:15 Japanese time, one plane drops one bomb (weight of uranium approximately 22 pounds) and vanishes a city. Eighty thousand people (more or less) killed at once, mainly through fire and blast; another 40,000 (more or less) dead within weeks from injuries, infections, and radiation.

1 atomic bomb = 1 city

Numbers float away, meanings evaporate. What can 40,000 charred people do to help themselves? What can doctors do when there are no nurses, hospitals, medicines, or doctors? When there is not even water?

A friend of mine, a navy surgeon, had a vivid encounter with nuclear magnitudes in Nagasaki. In 1945, after the Japanese surrender, his cruiser was to land some Marines and Seabees to occupy the bombed-out city and begin the clean-up. He was ordered in to see what remained of housing, water, electricity, transportation, communications, etc., for the occupying troops. He was also told to give what medical help he could.

This was six weeks after the bombing, but neither his skipper nor Navy Intelligence could tell him what to expect on shore. Here was a city bombed with one plutonium bomb. Reports had it that almost half of its 280,000 people had died in the first twelve hours, another 15 to 20 percent in the weeks thereafter.

It was low tide when the doctor went ashore, escorted by a pair of nervous Marines. The captain's gig landed them on a float at the bottom of a tall ships' wharf. A staircase of cement steps led to the top. What would they find up there? Would it be like Germany at the end, people living in makeshift caves in half-smashed buildings? Would there be gangs of hungry, desperate men, or angry Kamikazes determined to get one Yank before joining their ancestors?

Reaching the top of the wharf the doctor found the whole city opening out. Only it wasn't a city, it was nothing. For nearly two miles a plain of ash and rubble stretched away before him to some sharp green foothills. In the distance one sturdy lump of a building still stood, on a knoll beside the squashed steel webwork of the Mitsubichi torpedo plant.

Nothing moving. Not a person. Not a child running or a dog scrounging. No sounds. Only the lapping of bright morning waves against the boat landing below.

Perhaps Nagasaki and Hiroshima pushed us to the limits of comprehension. But at least we were still able to see a human dimension in those early nuclear numbers. Unfortunately, eight years after Hiroshima, the physicists (simultaneously in Russia and America) presented us with yet another new math, a hydrogen explosion, roughly a thousand times bigger still.

1 hydrogen bomb = 1,000 Hiroshima bombs

And where, pray, are the thousandfold cities? Moscow (8 million)? New York (9 million)? Two dozen old-fashioned Nagasaki bombs could take care of those toy cities.

II

Atomic explosions run to large numbers. In contrast, the aftermath, the fallout, the waste products of the chain reactions, may be dangerous in invisibly small amounts.

Plutonium, for example. Plutonium is a man-made metal deriving from uranium. It works well in A-bombs and serves as part of the trigger mechanism in H-bombs. The government hopes that plutonium will also prove manageable enough to work in the so-called breeder reactor — a new complicated power reactor which, in theory, breeds plutonium from uranium, then splits the plutonium to create heat, electricity, waste products, neutrons, and more plutonium.

Plutonium may not be the worst of man-made poisons, but a few pounds of it equally divided among all people on earth would kill every one with cancer.

There can be little doubt of this. Long ago in hundreds of tests, the effects of plutonium on experimental animals proved uniform and deadly. Mice injected under the skin with a few millionths of a gram of plutonium developed cancer in 100 percent of the cases. Plutonium in the air as a fine dust is to be feared even more. Just as uranium miners breathing small amounts of radon gas over a period of years tend to develop lung cancer, so do experimental dogs living in an atmosphere lightly contaminated by plutonium dust. In fact, researchers found no levels of plutonium oxide dust so small as to produce no cancers.

Other fission products, working in other ways, may be just as bad. A-bomb explosions and nuclear plants produce two or three hundred elements and isotopes, all radioactive, all potentially dangerous. *Cesium 137*, which is similar to potassium, gets into fleshy tissues, into fish, meat, nuts, fruits. The notorious *strontium 90* masquerades as calcium and so concentrates in milk, cheese, ice cream, and yogurt; in the body it goes to the bones.

Perhaps the most devilish of all the fission isotopes is *iodine 131*, created in large amounts in atomic explosions. It is readily absorbed into the blood, where it is picked up by the thyroid gland, exactly as though it were normal seawater iodine.

The worst iodine disasters happen to unborn babies. In the first three or four months of development, the embryo's whole job is to get safely from a one-celled being to a miniature human prototype. This miraculous process, which carries its small copy of the history of the race as well as blueprints for the future of the individual, is controlled after the seventh week of gestation by the embryo's tiny thyroid gland. An invasion of radioactive iodine at this juncture can wreck the process. Miscarriages and stillbirths are the kindest result. Too often the baby is born retarded, small-headed, deformed, crippled in some way.

We moved the people out of Bikini to the smaller, poorer atoll of Rongerik, promising to bring them back as soon as the tests were over. The tests, we said, were necessary "for the good of mankind and to end all wars." I think we meant those words. But things went wrong. The underwater explosion was much worse than expected, the poisoned ships had to be sunk, the islands quarantined. Then, in 1949, the Russians made their first A-bomb and the race to build a hydrogen bomb turned to a frenzy. Over the next 15 years, Bikini and Eniwetok atolls suffered 64 more nuclear tests.

Some of these were huge eruptions: whole islands disappeared, vaporized; coral reefs and coral sands in millions of tons were sucked into the sky, mixed with the swarming radioisotopes, and spread far and wide downwind on ocean and atoll, fish and palm and native population, wherever the gentle trade winds happened to blow.

Thus, in 1954, the people of Rongerik and Rongelap, Wotho, Likiep, and other islands saw their first snowstorm, falling as a fine coral sand out of the clouds from an explosion 125 miles away. Rongelap was showered for hours, the people severely burned by beta-gamma radiation on heads, hands, feet, eyelids, necks, shoulders, beltlines — anywhere the dust could catch and stick to sweaty skin. An emergency evacuation was organized three days later, the people being taken to Kwajalein, where they were examined and told there was "no significant danger."

No. Not then. Not visibly. The skin burns healed and the people returned to their islands. But later, on nearby Rongelap, 19 out of 22 children had to be operated on for thyroid nodules.

An even worse affliction was visited upon the people of the out-of-the-way atoll of Likiep: nine children were born retarded, ten others were abnormal in some way, and three babies were stillborn — one a monster reported to be "not recognizable as human."

The population of Likiep was 406.

Now that the atmospheric testing is over, Kwajalein, a very large atoll, has become the target end of a missile range. Target practice begins at Vandenberg Air Force Base in California, or aboard submarines in the Pacific: up go the big ICBM's and Poseidons, arching across four or five thousand miles of sky and homing in on designated islets in the Kwajalein chain.

Missiles are tracked and antimissile missiles are sent up to try to intercept the incoming war machines. (The Russians have the same kind of shooting range. They fire their big missiles from the Urals, or from the sea, toward targets on Kamchatka, a long isolated peninsula lying northeast of Japan. Each side can watch the other from its satellites and compute the range and accuracy.)

Since the Marshall Islands are far away, Washington has made only spasmodic efforts to clean up the bomb messes. On Eniwetok, for example, the worst of the poisoned sands were bulldozed off and placed in a bomb crater on Runit island, the whole huge dump then capped with cement.

Fishermen and food-gatherers are sternly warned away; Runit island is "off limits for 240,000 years." (Two hundred and forty thousand years is not exactly voodoo science. It equals ten half-lives of plutonium.) Of course, no native will wait. Nor would we. As soon as the soothsayers are gone, the people will be fishing and collecting coconuts as usual. But the warning comforts us in its meaninglessness. A quarter of a million years is 70 times farther away than the war of Troy; it is back in the second ice age before the advent of the Neanderthals.

Washington's science worked no better for the people of Rongelap. More than 20 years after they returned to their atoll they were told that they could no longer go to the northern group of islands. John Anjain, the local magistrate, wrote a kind of epitaph for his ill-fated people:

> We are told by the Department of Energy doctors not to eat food on the land and fish in the oceans near these islands. . . . We have been eating the food and living on these islands since the Atomic Energy Commission told us it was safe in 1957.

Anjain should know. He and two sons have had thyroid operations; one son recently died of leukemia.

Of all those South Sea atolls, surely Bikini was the fairest. It had palms and pandanus in abundance, fishing to spare, and a wide, serene harbor. To give up such a home for Rongerik, with its poison fish, or for Jabor, or Kili, which is a bare coast, was hardship indeed.

When at last, in the late 1960s, the Bikini people were told they could return, that "virtually no radiation" was left on the islands, the natives were understandably wary. Lied to, misled, abandoned and bamboozled for 25 years, they now demanded a full and independent radiation survey. The Americans instead promised free housing and food. (Bikinians had heard these promises before, heralding the move to Kili where they had, in a stormy season, barely escaped starvation.)

Eventually some hundred people returned to Bikini's ploughed and shredded islands. The topsoil had been bulldozed and dumped into the ocean; new palms had been planted. Stone Age people, simple fisher-gatherers, the Bikinians could comprehend little of what the Americans did, but now at least the Americans were gone.

Then in 1975 government scientists found the well water contaminated and "low levels of plutonium in the urine" of the natives. Experts solemnly pronounced the necessary words: "not radiologically significant." But further studies showed unexpected levels of strontium, and the palms to be "sopping up" cesium.

Finally, in 1978, the Bikini islanders were moved out again, some to the hated islands of their former exile, some to little Enyu at the entrance to the atoll. The people on Enyu were told that the main Bikini island would not be habitable for 30 years.

Then they were told they would have to evacuate Enyu, which itself would not be safe for 20 years.

Then they were told they could remain on Enyu provided they spent no more than 10 percent of their time on the main island and provided 50 percent of their food was imported.

Bikini is empty again. The children have wandered among the deserts of their tropical paradise for nearly 40 years and there is no end.

III

The innocents of Hiroshima, Nagasaki, and Bikini were soon to have company. In the 1950s and early 1960s, fevered by H-bombs and sputniks, we brought our testing home to a desert valley in southern Nevada called Yucca Flat. There for a decade we tested new models of bombs, big ones and small ones, nuclear artillery, mortars, and other devices. We brought in companies of soldiers and marines to let them lie out close to the explosions (2,000 yards) in order to train them in modern war conditions.

At the same time we entertained the local ranchers and villagers with dawn extravaganzas of light, color, sound, and nuclear cloud effects. We also dusted them with fine ash.

More than 90 tests were made. The little towns of Nevada, Utah, Arizona, and Montana became our Bikinis, Rongelaps, Rongeriks, and Likieps.

Sheep were the first casualties. Two dirty explosions in 1956 killed some 17,000 sheep. Among the remainder, almost half the lambs were stillborn, many showing weird deformities. The ranchers could prove nothing, and the government experts insisted that, with only 3.9 rads lying about, radiation could not be the cause of the mysterious epizootic. Then a doctor in St. Louis, finding high levels of iodine 131 in the local milk, traced the contamination back to Nevada. There he showed that sheep — munching on everything as they do — concentrated the fallout thousands of times in their guts and even more in their thyroid glands.

So too with the people. In due time residents of the little atoll towns of St. George, Enterprise, Cedar City, Parawan, Pleasant Grove, and Fredonia suffered malignancies like nothing anyone had seen before. Yet the people could do nothing to help themselves. They couldn't find out what was wrong. They couldn't measure for radiation in any reliable way; they couldn't test for iodine 131 or strontium or plutonium. The government's test results were secret. Cool and uncontaminated, the experts continued to say "no radiation of any significance . . ." or "not a single documented case . . ." or "about what you'd receive if you played golf in the sunshine. . . ."

A road of deceptions gets progressively washed out.

This one led to a complete cave-in over the veterans exposed to nuclear blasts. More than 260,000 soldiers and marines have been exposed; some have been in on several tests. When, 20 years later, veterans began to come down with the usual malignancies (or with the bizarre symptoms that go with extreme anxiety) they found they were turned away from V.A. hospitals; their symptoms were not "service connected." Nor could they get the records of their radiation exposure. Such information was reported to be secret, or to show nothing of consequence, or to be missing from the files, or accidentally lost in a fire in St. Louis.

War hysteria makes fools of us all.

Sometimes I wish our government could sit down with a dying veteran. It might better understand the true costs of its war games. It might at least resolve to run its atomic business with candor and with care.

Even more I wish it would sit down with a leukemic child or two. As parents and nurses and doctors know, there is something special about such children. An aura, a feeling. We catch a glimmer of that quality in the way they look: lashes extra long, eyes large and dark with a kind of midnight seeing. In a slow terrible smelter, a purification is going on. Such children are always strong, gentle, enduring, brave. They seem to be looking back at us from some other place, as though to tell us something. But we don't know how to listen. Then they are gone. We never quite find out what it was.

IV

Are we next? It may come by stealth. It may come as an accident in a power plant or a storage plant, such as the Russians had at Kyshtym, such as we nearly had at Detroit and Three Mile Island. It may come by computer mistake or human error or political blundering. So many people have been victimized and brushed aside by us in our panicky drive for nuclear superiority that surely one day we shall be called to account.

Panic it must be. The number of bombs we have piled up for national security has blotted out numbers and all sense of security. The people on this earth are fewer than the tons of explosives by one to four.

Worse than this, our policies have driven adults into apathy and stolen hope from young people.

Calmly, sanely, we talk about a war that is insane, about a war which would make the exterminations of Auschwitz seem like a whiff of laughing gas in a dentist's chair. For what would be the reality of a thermonuclear war? No one can adequately describe those immense multiple explosions much less foretell the human environment that would follow the falling of thousands of such thunderbolts.

The physicist Philip Morrison asks us to imagine, for a single 1-megaton bomb, a freight train loaded with boxes of TNT. The train would be 250 miles long; it would trundle by for six to eight hours while we watched and counted the cars.

For a giant H-bomb, 15 million tons in size, the freight train wouldn't be able to move: its engines would be in New York City, and its caboose in San Francisco.

But where in the world are the cities so big and so sinful as to require chastisement from 3,000 miles of boxcars of TNT?

Let us consider some of the nuclear targets, cities the size of Hiroshima or larger.

USA		USSR	
New York	(9.1 million)	Moscow	(8.4 million)
Los Angeles	(7.5)	Leningrad	(4.5)
Chicago	(7.1)	Kiev	(2.7)
Philadelphia	(4.7)	Tashkent	(1.8)
Detroit	(4.4)	Baku	(1.5)
San Francisco/Oakland	(3.3)	Kharkov	(1.4)
Washington, D.C.	(3.1)	Gorki	(1.3)
Dallas/Fort Worth	(3)	Novosibirsk	(1.3)
Houston	(3)	Minsk	(1.3)
Boston	(2.8)	Kuibyshev	(1.2)
Nassau	(2.8)	Sverdlovsk	(1.2)
St. Louis	(2.6)	Dnepropetrovsk	(1.1)
Baltimore	(2.6)	Tbilisi	(1.1)
Minneapolis/St. Paul	(2.4)	Odessa	(1.1)
Atlanta	(2.2)	Chelyabinsk	(1.1)
Newark	(2.2)	Donetsk	(1)
Anaheim	(2)	Yerovan	(1)
		Omsk	(1)

108 more cities		71 more cities	
Omaha	(303,000)	Samarkand	(304,000)
Total: 126 cities		Total: 90 cities	

216 cities in all, for which, against which, we and the Russians have stockpiled some 18,000 A- and H-bombs.

Another way to state the absurdity of our present nuclear stockpile is this:

> *If all our megatonnage were in Hiroshima-sized bombs, we could drop one a day since the time of Christ and still not run out.*
> *The Russians could do the same.**

Bomb Samarkand? Go slow! It was an ancient center before Ghengis Khan lived there and Marco Polo passed by. Relics of relatives of ours are thereabouts, the bones of some of our smartest ancestors. They lived along the shore of an inland sea and were among the first people who learned to plant and care for seeds.

That was only a short time ago, some 8,000 or 9,000 years. Compared with the rest of the human adventure, or just the last million years of it, the learning of agriculture seems an easy, simple thing. It was, in fact, a mighty innovation. It asked us to learn things we had no preparation for: to stay in one place, to plant and tend and harvest, to store and select the seed, to work together, planning for the year to come. Culture began with cultivation.

No greater test have we passed except possibly learning to survive four ages of ice. Fortunately those early planters had the wit to learn and the time to let nature instruct them.

---

* This is figuring 300 days per year. We shouldn't bomb people on Sundays, Thanksgiving, Christmas, New Year's, Veterans Day, Bank Day, etc.

Samarkand? Omaha? Playing games with abstract cities makes us dangerous to everyone. Recently a civil defense authority in Washington, contemplating survival in a nuclear war, proclaimed that "if we have enough shovels, everyone will make it."

We have heard it all before, first after the Russians began testing their atom bombs, later after the Cuban missile crisis. Now we have to hear it again because of the big SS-20s.

The missile crisis of 20 years ago should have taught us all we need to know. It began in October 1962, when highflying U2 planes photographed Russian missiles and missile launchers being set up in Cuba. Stunned disbelief was our first reaction: War? Atomic war? Over what?

The idea spooked us. It made no difference that we had ships and planes the Russians could not begin to match on this side of the Atlantic. It made no difference that we already had four times as many missiles planted around Russia — in Scotland, England, Turkey, Japan, and elsewhere — as the Russians had in Cuba . . .

For a moment, we Americans had a look (not a very close look) at the realities of nuclear war, ourselves on the receiving end. What we constantly threaten to do to others was now perhaps to be done to us.

One could guess a little from the experience at Hiroshima and Nagasaki, but not very much. Those were single explosions of small bombs. What a skyful of thermonuclear bombs would do raining down more or less simultaneously no one could begin to predict. Fifty million people engulfed and buried and burned in their cities. Twenty million more, battered and broiled. What then?

One drizzly afternoon, our children came running home to announce that the whole school had had a "bomb practice." That is, in each room when the bell rang the teacher and children lay down and put their heads under the desks.

For the boys, any nutty exercise was welcome diversion from schoolwork; for the girls it was yukky and frightening. The smallest girl asked the biggest question: "But why bomb kids? We didn't do anything."

We discussed over supper what we should do if the planes and missiles started flying. First a fallout shelter: we'd bust through the cellar foundation and carve out a good-sized cave, big enough for all eight of us. If the clouds came our way, from Troy and Albany, Buffalo and Rochester, we'd have to stay underground two or three weeks, maybe much longer. We could keep food nearby in boxes and cans, water in jugs and in the bathtub. But how to keep the baby, a two-year-old, imprisoned in the cave for three weeks? Nor did we ever figure out the details of an inhouse outhouse.

But those were only the minor problems of one family pretending they would soon be returning to the good old world. The truth would be far different. We would need tools, and all tools would be gone from the stores within a week: axes, saws, shovels, hoes, picks, nails, pails, rope, knives, bore-holers (we would learn to value tools as the Stone Age people had) — and food (the stores would be empty in two days) — wool clothing, heavy pants and shirts, long underwear, thick socks, mitts, boots (our boys could run through a pair of boots in four wet months) — and bandages, aspirin, vaseline — and needles, precious needles — and soap and matches . . .

Complicated, getting set up to live the simple aboriginal life again.

Our problems in the country would be nothing compared with those facing the survivors of the bombed cities. Millions of corpses, billions of rats, stink, insects, typhus, plague. The water filthy with debris, death, fallout, human sewage, dysentery, typhoid, cholera. Few nurses and doctors, almost no medicine, little to do to stave off the epidemics, nothing to do for the burn victims. (The doctor who suggested that all civil defense funds be put into stockpiling morphine was a lot closer to the truth than the cheerful shovel advocate.) With the rapid decline of all food supplies, starvation must soon follow.

Seeds. Seeds would be life itself. I reckoned we could get by the first winter, but spring would be hard when things were growing but nothing was ready to eat. I couldn't see beyond the second winter. The second winter might prove to be an impossible test.

I found myself angry with the politicians for having

played tic-tac-toe with our lives and angry with myself for having paid so little attention.

Day after day the crisis seemed to get worse. President Kennedy sent out the navy, complete with submarines and aircraft; still the Russian ships kept coming on. I began to believe that, in spite of the absurdities, this game might suddenly turn serious.

The little girl and I went down to the country store to lay in a supply of seeds. The clerk found a few remaining from summer, pathetic little envelopes of radishes and lettuce and carrots, and various flowers. That made the girl happy; the flowers would look beautiful in spring and besides, they were mother's favorites.

But of real food, survival food — beans, corn, squash — there was no seed to be had. And no potatoes. I asked the clerk if he had any seed potatoes stowed out back. No, he said. Not 'till spring; he always got a shipment of seed potatoes in the spring. The potatoes out front in the store were no good, he said; they had been treated with some kind of chemical to keep them from germinating.

So there we were, limp beneficiaries of modern agribusiness, unequipped to survive as the clever Neanderthals had. We would probably be better off than the city folk for a while; but in the end we would all face the same Darwinian environment. By the second winter, if not before, starvation, murder, and cannibalism would become commonplace.

Not a great exit scene for 8,000 years of civilization.

Fortunately when freighters met cruisers at last, two hundred miles off the Cuban coast, the Russians turned their vessels back and the crisis passed. I gave thanks to our neighbors for their good sense. I also resolved never to be without a sharp axe and working potatoes again.

The confrontation wasn't over, of course. The experience in 1962 seemed to confirm for Americans their slogan that "Russians understand nothing but power." As for the Russians, they quietly swore to themselves to build such weapons that never again could the Americans make them back down. These hardline policies on both sides have brought us to our present weapons impasse.

V

. . . I think over again
My small adventures
When an off-shore wind blew me out
In my kayak
And I thought I was lost.

My fears,
Those small fears
That I thought so big
For all the vital things
I had to get and reach . . .

And yet there is only
One great thing,
The only thing:
To live to see from huts or camps
The day that dawns
The great light that fills the world.
                    —GREENLAND ESKIMO

My particular small adventure came on me quite gently
one day when I was splitting up the winter's wood; next
morning I saw clotted blood as black and gray spots in
the sky, and occasional bursts of lightning. There was no
problem in diagnosis: detached retinas.

In any other era the doctors would have sandbagged
my head for a couple of months, warned me not to
cough or sneeze or go to the bathroom, and then I would
have either recovered somewhat or gone on to blindness.
But now, with modern medical technology and with la-
ser beams and frozen nitrogen for spot welding, the
probabilities have all changed.

Mapping of the inner geography of my eyes, surveyed by remarkable light machines, was an adventure
in itself. I was dissociated, refracted, picked up and scattered among the wild colors of the spectrum. It was like
being present when all the wavelengths were tested and
fitted together, when at last the words were spoken:
"Let there be Light."

After that came the welding, requiring the highest

kind of skill by surgeon and anesthetist. Released from the hospital some days later, I knew exactly how I wanted to celebrate my restored vision: with a big plate of quahogs and a goodly slug of vodka.

My wife thought I was having some sort of drug reaction, but the explanation was simple: having had the best of modern technology and surgical skill, I wanted to get back to the most primitive and enduring of the life-sustaining gifts, the clams of the shore and the spiritus of the good earth. I wanted to sit once more on that raw shore to which we had come first as lungfish 300 million years ago, later as fishermen and seed planters, finally as Greeks and Eskimos and nuclear physicists.

In the darkness of my post-op days, I had had ample time to reflect on the perilous journey we humans had made. The miracles of our naked survival among the big animals and centuries of ice seemed no fitting prelude to a stupid or mistaken extinction by our own hands.

Memory, imagination, and speech — those three — had brought us through two million years, through from caves and campfires to the genius and dependencies of civilization. Bombs would save nothing.

Clearly our race was coming to one of its great crossings. We would have to go ahead on faith and begin the new path with not much more than instinct to guide us and courage to sustain us. The choice was rather plain: we would learn to bear each other or we would bury each other.

I wanted to sit on the shore and say to that fellow across the water:

Come, Ivan. Let us try again. Let us stop shouting, agree to stop building bombs for three years, and make some plans.

Like it or not, we have both already pledged our lives, our fortunes, and our sons and daughters, so let us go on from there.

Look, our difficulties are all man-made, made by us. They can't be nearly as hard to get through as an ice age. So let us meet and try again. I'll bring the quahogs. You bring the vodka.

1983   D. B.

A GUIDE TO THE DANGERS OF RADIOACTIVITY

RADIOACTIVITY is not something new. Life as it evolved on this earth has been accustomed to, if not aware of, definite amounts of radiation. We are subjected to a constant shower of cosmic rays from the heavens, and to a lesser barrage from radioactive materials present on the surface of the earth. Some of the heaviest elements, like uranium and thorium, belong to the group of "radioactive elements." These elements appear to be unsuited to nature's economy. Little by little, and according to a constant pattern, they are breaking up into smaller elements; in so doing they give off small particles, and units of energy known as rays, until at last they find a stable and satisfactory configuration.

Thus, for example, uranium passes through a series of transformations, down through radium the metal, and radon the gas, and at last, thousands of years later, reaches its end point, lead. (See Figure 5 in the following pages.) Each change is a complete transformation, resulting in the formation of an entirely different element; the release of energy and mass is in the form of "radiation." This process is called "decay"; once initiated the decay proceeds at a rate wholly uninfluenced by factors of temperature, pressure, and so on. We know of no way to stop or to speed up this decay rate. Certain stages endure but fractions of seconds; others last for tens of centuries.

An interesting by-product of studies in radioactive decay is the geologists' time clock. Since the process of decay proceeds according to a pattern as well known and predictable as the cycles of the moon, one school of thought holds that it is possible, by studying the relative concentrations of decay products in uranium ore, to work back to a theoretical time when, of unstable elements, there was only pure uranium on the earth. This is estimated to be roughly not more than 3 billion, 400 million years ago. What the precursors of uranium were and under what conditions they existed cannot be said, but at least it gives some hint as to the finite existence of the earth.

So much for naturally occurring radiation. With the development of machines like the cyclotron it has been possible to pack the nuclei of certain elements with extra particles, mainly neutrons, without changing their chemical identity. Thus an "isotope" is created.

Such an atom is thrown into a state of abnormal agitation. It is like a family when the in-laws suddenly move in. Seeking the peace and serenity of the old order, this overcharged atom has two alternatives: either it will give off the unaccustomed factors, along with the release of energy in the form of radiation, or it will pick up other balancing factors (electrons) and settle down to an entirely different existence.

Types

The radiation mentioned may be of several forms, but of these only four types are of significance as a potential danger to life.

1. *The Alpha Particle:* this is the nucleus of a helium atom, divested of its orbital electrons. They are relatively enormous and so are stopped almost at once by collisions with molecules of the air. They cannot penetrate the skin or even pass through paper and so are not dangerous outside of the body. However, if they emanate from substances lodged within the body, especially within the bone marrow, they can do great damage and even prove ultimately fatal. They are produced by many radioactive substances, notably uranium, radium, and plutonium.

2. *The Beta Particles:* these are high-speed electrons. Their mass is almost negligible, and they too have little penetrating power. They too will be dangerous if given off within the body.

3. *The Gamma Rays:* these are ultrashort electromagnetic waves, closely related to X rays. Depending upon their energy, they have great penetrating power and constitute the main hazard from radiation outside the body.

4. *Neutrons:* all atoms larger than the smallest, hydrogen, have nuclei made up of two constituents — protons, with a positive electrical charge that balances the negative charges of the electrons in the orbits outside the nucleus, and neutrons, which are about the same size, but possess no electrical charge.

Neutrons are released in the process of splitting an atom (fission), and they are the agents which make a chain reaction possible. Thus they are being constantly produced in the operation of an atomic "pile," and are momentarily present in countless numbers during an atomic explosion.

Neutrons are very deadly. Being uncharged and traveling at high speeds, they find the skin no barrier. It takes feet of water or cement to stop them. Their action upon the lightweight atoms which make up body tissues is a little like cueing off a pool game with an .88 shell. In three ways neutrons can damage and destroy:

1. They produce enormous numbers of ions in whatever medium they pass through. In colliding with other atoms they knock off orbital electrons, thus changing or "ionizing" those atoms. Any tissue which has its constituents sufficiently ionized will die.

2. They excite secondary beta and gamma radiations from substances with which they collide.

3. When absorbed into the nuclei of other atoms they result in the production of the aforementioned "radioactive isotopes." That is what is meant by "induced radioactivity."

It is likely that most of the damage done specifically by *radiation* to the inhabitants of Hiroshima and Nagasaki was done by neutrons. The majority of alpha, beta, and gamma producing materials, the by-products of the explosion, was carried up into the stratosphere in the now familiar cloud.

Detection

All these forms of radiation are more real in the mumbo-jumbo world of the physicist than they are to most of us. They are too small to be seen or felt, too stealthy to be heard or smelled. But the disturbance they make in their environment can be detected in many ways: by the fogging of photographic film; by the comet's tail of ionized particles in a Wilson cloud chamber; by the discharging of an electroscope; by the clicks of electrical discharges in a Geiger counter.

It is perfectly clear that nature had no intention that any of her children should be monkeying around with radioactive elements, else she would have provided us with some sixth sense to protect us from running headlong into dangerous amounts of radiation. No, she evidently expected us to take our daily dose of cosmic and earth's radiation as we take the cuts and bruises of ordinary living. The idea of getting them out in the form of concentrated extracts was man's, and since the day when the Curies isolated radium from pitchblende, men have had to extend their perceptive capacities by means of various devices.

The earliest device, which indeed first aroused the Curies to pioneer the wilderness of radioactivity, was the fogging of photographic emulsion. Today it is still a very practical method of detecting radiation and is used universally by people working with radioactivity. Film, of course, is no good as a warning device. It can merely tell you later, when developed and compared to a standard, how much radiation you have been exposed to.

A second method of detecting radiation is by means of an electroscope. There are many kinds and modifications of electroscopes ranging from the simple gold-leaf device of high-school days to the neat and compact quartz fibre Lauritsen electroscopes. Their mode of action is simple. They must first be charged to a standard potential; once charged they pick up the ionized particles left in the wake of a passing beta particle or gamma ray, and we may observe their progressive discharge as long as any radiation or charge on the scope remains. Since the rate of discharge is proportional to the degree of ionization a rough estimate of the radioactivity can be obtained. Unfortunately, the electroscope does not tell of present radiation, but only of past radiation, giving the summation of innumerable little discharges.

In order to measure the degree of radioactivity at a particular moment one needs some sort of radiation meter, the most famous of which is the Geiger-Müller counter. Basically the Geiger counter is a sort of electroscope. It must be charged before it can record, and what it records is the momentary discharge in its circuits resulting from an influx of ionized particles. These discharges are amplified through a series of circuits and tubes so delicate as to make the workings of a Swiss watch seem on a par with a cement mixer.

FUNDAMENTALS OF ATOMIC PHYSICS

As far as we know today all matter is made up of combinations of these building blocks:

> The electron — the unit of electricity, having one negative electrical charge.
>
> The proton — 1800 times as large, having one positive electrical charge.
>
> The neutron — about the size of a proton, having no charge. (The neutron may be a combination of a proton and an electron.)

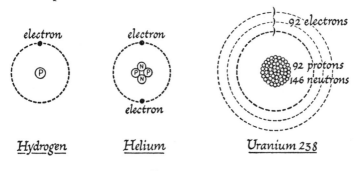

Figure 1

Other small units are recognized, namely the positron or "positive electron"; the meson, long suspected and recently proven particle intermediate in size between the electron and the proton; and the tiny elusive neutrino, present in spirit at least to satisfy the laws of mass and energy.

Atoms are composed of a nucleus of protons and neutrons, surrounded by "orbital" electrons much as the earth and other planets swing in their orbits about the sun.

Earth's Radioactivity

Many forms of radiant energy are familiar to us, among them heat, light, ultraviolet light, radio waves, and X rays. Radioactivity naturally occurring on earth is principally of three kinds: alpha, beta, gamma. Since they bear differing electrical charges and masses they may be separated by passing them through a magnetic field. In the same way, neutrons, positrons, and protons may also be separated.

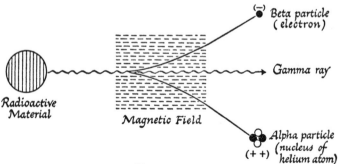

Figure 2

Fission

When a neutron collides with the nucleus of an unstable atom, that nucleus may be set into such agitation as to fly apart into smaller pieces, known as "fission products." One or more neutrons are also released. Energy too is released, namely some of the nuclear binding energy which previously held the large unstable nucleus unwillingly together. The energy of an atomic explosion is this excess of nuclear binding energy given off as countless billions of unstable atoms undergo fission in a matter of a few millionths of a second.

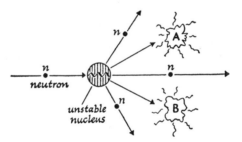

Figure 3

Fission products A and B are themselves in a high state of agitation and must give off this energy in the form of radioactivity.

A Chain Reaction

This occurs when the neutrons produced by fission of one nucleus excite fission in neighboring unstable nuclei. It looks simple on paper, but getting the conditions just right is the trick.

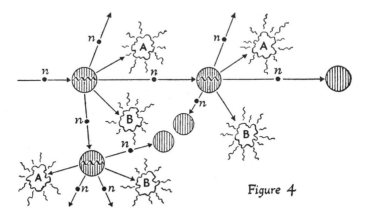

Figure 4

In an *atomic bomb* the chain reaction is complete in a fraction of a second. The energy released in that instant is enormous.

In an *atomic pile* the chain reaction proceeds more slowly. It is a controlled explosion which may be hastened or stopped. The energy released is similarly under control and theoretically could be used to benefit mankind.

Half Life

Radioactive elements decay at a definite and predictable rate. Each material has its own characteristic decay rate over which it is completely sovereign.

The half life is merely a convenient way of expressing

how long it will take the process of radioactive decay to reduce an unstable element to one half of its original amount.

The half life of uranium 238 is four billion years.

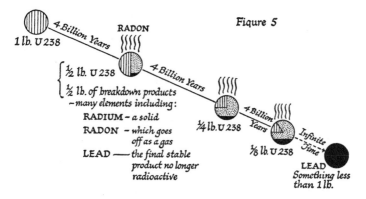

Figure 5

1 lb. U 238 — 4 Billion Years — RADON

½ lb. U 238
½ lb. of breakdown products
— many elements including:
RADIUM — a solid
RADON — which goes off as a gas
LEAD — the final stable product no longer radioactive

4 Billion Years — ¼ lb. U 238 — 4 Billion Years — ⅛ lb. U 238 — Infinite Time — LEAD Something less than 1 lb.

Carbon 12 — carbon in its normal state.

Carbon 11 — half life of 20 minutes.

Carbon 14 — half life of 5,700 years.

This illustrates the wide variation in rate of radioactive decay and suggests the danger from lingering radioactivity following the use of atomic weapons.

BIOLOGICAL EFFECTS OF RADIATION

1. A radioactive particle or ray in passing through a medium, be it gaseous or solid, has numerous collisions with atoms of that medium and leaves behind it a wake of ionized fragments.

It is these ions, positively and negatively charged particles, which are detected by the Geiger-Müller counters.

The capacity of a radioactive particle to ionize depends upon its size and electrical charge and speed. Over a given distance of track a slower-moving particle will make more hits and cause greater ionization, but of course over the total track the faster-moving particle, having more energy, will have more ionizing power.

A beta particle, being small and having only one negative charge, will not be able to ionize as heavily as an alpha particle, bearing two positive charges and having a mass over 7000 times as great. The alpha particle however has so many collisions it is brought to a stop almost at once.

A neutron, having large mass, no charge, and traveling at enormous speeds, will cause considerable stir over a great distance. The great damage from neutrons, however, is not so much from the primary ionization, as from the ionizing power of innumerable fragments of atoms left in its wake.

2. The damage done in living tissue by the passage of radioactive particles or rays is a result of the ionization produced.

If enough atoms are ionized, the molecule, as part of a living mechanism, is destroyed.

If enough molecules are injured the cell is destroyed.

If enough cells are injured the living mechanism cannot survive.

3. Bacteria fight according to the Marquis of Queens-

The Dangers of Radioactivity

Type	Nature	Effect	Danger	Detection
Gamma Rays	Non-particulate Similar to X rays	Travels great distances Passes easily through body	Both at time of explosion and from fission products evolved	Fairly accurately measured by the Geiger counter
Beta Particles	An electron	Ionization small Usually stopped by first layers of skin	Mainly when emitted inside of body	Fairly accurately measured by Geiger counter
Neutron	1800 times size of electron	Travels great distances. Passes through body. Heavy secondary ionization.	Produced at moment of explosion and constantly by pile	Must be measured indirectly
Alpha Particles	Nucleus of helium atom	Heavy brief ionization Easily stopped by skin	Only when emitted within the body as with radium and plutonium	Requires special very delicate counter

Figure 6

berry rules. With them it is direct invasion of the organism by means of well-accepted weapons such as toxins. With radioactivity it is the impersonal and mathematical production of ionization against which the body has no defense.

In either case there is a limit of injury beyond which the organism cannot recover.

ADDENDA TO GUIDE

Matter

The building blocks of matter (pp. 175-176) seemed fairly well understood in 1946. Now I read of leptons and quarks, hadons, muons, gluons, down, up, strange, and charm and wonder whether this is physics or a new book by Lewis Carroll.

Rads, Rems, etc.

At Bikini, we used the standard measurement for radiation — roentgens — developed over many years by X ray specialists. Modern biophysicists adapt this unit to varying purposes.

> *curie:* nuclear disintegrations as the radioactive material "decays." (1 curie = 37 billion disintegrations per second per gram of radium. You can imagine what a bombardment is going on when even so little as a millionth of a gram is lodged in the bones.)

> *roentgen:* a measure of energy causing ionization. A not inconsiderable result. 1 r. produces approximately 2 billion ion pairs in human tissue.

rem: roentgen equivalent for man. Man — human cellular material — is the substance here being ionized.

rad: roentgen absorbed dose. The dose actually absorbed by cells; 100 ergs per gram of tissue.

For practical purposes, however, the rad and rem are roughly equal to the roentgen.

Is there a safe level of radiation?

No. Any dose is potentially damaging and the damage is approximately equal to the dose. "Background radiation" is unavoidable; we couldn't escape it, even by going to live in a lead mine, for the rocks would irradiate us mildly every day and small amounts of radon would be there for us to breathe. Certain limits are imposed on us by nature; in between we think we make our own rules. Thus:

The normal background dose is about 0.1 rems per year, or 7 rems for an average lifetime.

The permitted maximum for workers in nuclear industries is 5 rems per year. (This seems small, yet in 20 years the accumulated dose of 100 rems ranks high in the range of significance.)

At 50 rems total-body-radiation (t.b.r.) most people will feel nauseous and ill temporarily.

At 200 rems t.b.r. some people will die.

At 500 rems t.b.r. almost all people will die.

These are some of the radiation conditions under which we live. Such words as "acceptable dose" or "allowable exposure" represent economic, not scientific, standards. If people are going to work in the nuclear business, they are going to have to work at above background levels. The important questions are: How much above background for how long? What's in the air and water? Do the workers know?

At Bikini, under quasi-military conditions, our standard was necessarily set much higher than 5 rems per year. We tried to keep the naval boarding parties within a "safe" maximum (0.1 of a roentgen per day), but our electroscopes were often in trouble from the salt, and we had no way of testing what was in the air. Since fallout is rarely uniform but comes down in hot spots, about all we could use were general averages and common sense.

Dr. Larson and I, flying in the first surveys over the target area, had an agreement between us that if we ran into radiation of 30 to 50 roentgens per hour, we would ask the pilot to turn away upwind and radio for instructions. In the underwater test we actually did bail out, not so much because we feared 50 r., but because we knew that down at water level that radiation would fry us all in minutes.

Obviously all notions of safe or reasonably safe levels of exposure would go by the board in even a limited nuclear war. We would struggle to survive, in ashes and in radiation, without help or succor, in numbers and in circumstances even the Japanese can't imagine.

"*Atom Bomb Disease*"

This was the name given to the events that overtook some of the Japanese. It is a misnomer; there is little that is disease-like in the radiation syndromes. Radiation is energy; its effects are mechanical and predictable, like being hit by a truck. Radiation destroys. It destroys in proportion to the amount, there being no known "threshold" or safe level and no immunity. While recovery occurs from medium and even large doses, some deep damage remains in the cells which may show up years later. Finally, children, especially babies in the womb, are much more sensitive to radiation than are adults.

These are some of the obvious characteristics of radiation. Yet the subject still seems spooky, partly because of the magnitude of the injuries in Japan, partly because we have no human detection system or natural defenses. Moreover, the effects of radiation show up in widely differing ways depending upon the kind of radiation, how much, whether received externally or internally, what kinds of cells or organs are primarily affected, and over what period of time.

In simple terms, there are two general groups of symptoms: the immediate, acute effects of radiation and the delayed, long-range probabilities.

Acute Radiation Syndrome

This is the familiar pattern of symptoms seen among certain of the survivors in Hiroshima and Nagasaki — those who escaped the blast and flash and firestorm but who were close enough to catch the gamma rays and neutrons. It would be typical of people caught in heavy fallout from a nuclear war or from a power plant meltdown.

(1) Immediate: nausea, vomiting, shock. Death may occur.
(2) Latent period (2 days to 2 weeks): apparent recovery; patient feels well.
(3) Acute symptoms appear (2 weeks to 3 months): fever, loss of hair, bleeding under skin, severe bloody diarrhea, very low red and white blood count.
(4) Recovery or demise.

The Japanese experience was complicated by mechanical injuries, burns, infections, lack of food, water, medicine or medical attention; yet it is surprising how consistently acute injuries followed this pattern. The same pattern was seen twice at Los Alamos, under good test conditions, when two people got caught in accidental bursts of neutrons and gamma radiation.

The second of the two, Dr. Louis Slotin, we Bikini doctors had known personally. He had taken us into his lab at Los Alamos to show us his experiments computing critical mass. A slender, intense man, he seemed to look on his work with an ironic detachment. Once he tossed us half an A-bomb — I suppose that is what it was, heavy as lead and about the size of half a tennis ball.

One day he pushed some pieces of plutonium too close together and crossed the invisible fatal line of critical mass. Instantly the air around was ionized blue. Yet he felt nothing. He had the odd sensation afterwards of knowing he was a dead man still walking around.

Louis passed through the initial nausea period and on to the state of feeling well again. But the mathematics of his accident were all against him. The best of medical care was available — blood, drugs, nursing, etc. — and specialists from all over the country were flown in to consult. Nothing mattered a whit. Right on schedule Louis Slotin completed the checklist and died.

Delayed Radiation Effects

These are the familiar long-range injuries we have seen among the Japanese, the Marshall Islanders, and ourselves.

(1) Genetic defects: miscarriages, stillbirths, neonatal deaths, retarded and deformed babies, sterility.

(2) Malignancies: after 8–12 years: leukemias; after 15–30 years: cancers and sarcomas.

Among the malignancies most commonly associated with radiation are the following: cancer of the lung, cancer of the breast, and malignant melanoma of the skin; leukemia, lymphoma, multiple myeloma, polycythemia; cancer of the salivary glands, esophagus, stomach, pancreas, liver, colon, and rectum; adenomas and cancers of the thyroid gland; cancer of the reproductive organs.

Cancer production is by no means the exclusive property of radiation. Any industrialized society will have a wide inventory of carcinogenic agents. Many of these are useful chemicals; some are by-products and waste products. We haven't learned to manage these dangerous chemicals very well, and for a country forty years into the atomic life-style, we haven't learned to pay attention to the details of radiation either.

Cancer-Doubling Dose

We used to think of 50 roentgens as being a fairly small dose of radiation, only enough to make you feel a little queasy. However, a series of excellent studies in England and elsewhere have drawn an entirely new picture. The amount of radiation that will double the normal rate of cancer in adults and experimental animals is approximately this:

30 r. for breast cancer

40 r. for leukemia

70 r. for lung cancer

90 r. for stomach and colon cancer

Young children, it turns out, may be ten times more susceptible to radiation damage than are adults. And babies in the first three or four months in utero may be fifty to a hundred times more susceptible.

One of the mysteries of life is the long delay before the onset of malignancy. What holds the damage back, containing it, smothering it for so long a time? Some sort of biological response is going on, some self-protective mechanism is being called on to hold off the invader — and so it does for a decade or two or three until for some reason control is lost and cell growth goes wild.

Carbon 14

The great physicists, like Bohr and Einstein, had more to fear than just an arms race with Russia. The whole circumstance of life on this planet is being called into question by the possibilities of atomic war.

We would be wise not to be too glib with our answers. The final statement may come from something we don't know about or have overlooked: the tiny, man-made isotope of carbon, for example. Carbon 14, is produced in enormous amounts in nuclear and thermo-nuclear explosions.

Carbon, of course, is fundamental to the chemistries of life. Will carbon 14 (half life 5,700 years) then enter the living cells like any other carbon? Who knows, for sure? At least three great scientists of our time — Andrei Sakharov in Russia, and Hans Bethe and Linus Pauling in this country — independently came to the conclusion that atomic war, flooding life with radio-active carbon, might "make life impossible."

It's not an experiment I want to make on life, a solitary spark (so far as we know) among the numberless lights and queer electrical sounds of black space.

LIBRARY OF CONGRESS CATALOGING IN PUBLICATION DATA

Bradley, David, 1915–
  No place to hide, 1946/1984.

  Originally published: 1948.
  1. Operation Crossroads. 2. Atomic bomb—Physiologi-
cal effect. 3. Bradley, David, 1915– . 4. Physi-
cians—United States—Biography. 5. Bikini Atoll
(Pacific Islands) I. Title.
U264.B73 1983   355'.0217   83-40013
ISBN 0-87451-274-3
ISBN 0-87451-275-1 (pbk.)